Grammarso

THE
ULTIMATE
GUIDE

TO TEACHING NON-FICTION WRITING, SPELLING, PUNCTUATION AND GRAMMAR

Photocopiable Resources
KS2

MITCH HUDSON
ANNA RICHARDS

BLOOMSBURY EDUCATION

LONDON OXFORD NEW YORK NEW DELHI SYDNEY

BLOOMSBURY EDUCATION

Bloomsbury Publishing Plc

50 Bedford Square, London, WC1B 3DP, UK

29 Earlsfort Terrace, Dublin 2, Ireland

BLOOMSBURY, BLOOMSBURY EDUCATION and the Diana logo are trademarks of Bloomsbury Publishing Plc

First published in Great Britain, 2021, by Bloomsbury Publishing Plc

Material from Department for Education documents used in this publication is approved under an
Open Government licence: www.nationalarchives.gov.uk/doc/open-government-licence/version/3

A catalogue record for this book is available from the British Library

ISBN: PB 978-1-4729-8833-1; ePDF 978-1-4729-8834-8

2 4 6 8 10 9 7 5 3 1

Cover design by James Fraser
Text design by Jeni Child

Printed and bound in the UK by CPI Group Ltd, Croydon CR0 4YY

To find out more about our authors and books visit www.bloomsbury.com and sign up for our newsletters

Dedications

For the three teachers who ignited my passion for the English language – Miss Capewell,
Mrs Holland and Miss Porter – and for my parents, Janice and Ian,
who always taught me to work the very hardest for my dreams.
Mitch

For my parents who taught me that education is the most important and powerful weapon in life;
to my husband, Dan, and darling daughter, Rosie, for being my world;
and to my co-author, Mitch, who made this dream a reality.
Anna

Contents

Introduction

Anna

Mitch

🐾 **As teachers**, we often searched for texts to use in the classroom and struggled to find ones that were of a high quality and appropriate for the children we were teaching: either they didn't have the right grammar coverage, the context wasn't appropriate, or the children had already studied the text in a different year group! This wasn't just our own experience, as we also witnessed this when working with other teachers in our school and in other school settings in our roles as SLEs and moderators.

We felt that teachers would benefit from a book which would allow them to easily access high-quality texts which were both age-appropriate and contained the relevant writing, grammar, spelling and punctuation from the National Curriculum and the teacher assessment frameworks. We strongly believe that these skills should be taught in context, rather than in standalone grammar or punctuation lessons.

Equally, we knew that grammar could be fun! We wanted to make sure that the texts we wrote were engaging for children of all ages and linked to the topics featured in the National Curriculum.

The Grammarsaurus website has always had a strong community spirit, with our followers helping to make key decisions such as the design of the logo, the colour scheme for the website, and even the title of the Grammarsaurus books. Therefore, it seemed right that our followers decided the topics the texts would focus on via an online poll.

The texts cover a range of contexts and topics: factual and imaginative, historical and current. Whilst the texts were written for particular year groups, you can use them for the other year groups too. They can be adapted to suit different year groups or used as inspiration to write your own.

We understand the confusion and uncertainty that sometimes surrounds 'working at a greater depth' as mentioned in the teacher assessment frameworks at the end of Key Stages 1 and 2. This is why we have included two texts for Year 6: one at the 'expected standard' and one at 'greater depth'.

We hope this book will support you when deciding what skills to teach and when. We ourselves use our text-specific overviews and model texts when planning: they are invaluable to us, and we hope they will become invaluable to you, too! The overviews will help you to decide when to teach different skills and the model texts will show how these skills can be used in different contexts. Whether you use the model texts to support your own knowledge or share them with your pupils to expose them to high-quality texts, we are sure they will be a great support.

How to use this book

Each chapter of this book focuses on a different non-fiction text type: instructional texts, explanation texts, non-chronological reports, recounts (diary), recounts (newspaper) and persuasive texts. Each chapter contains the following:

🦖 Teaching tips

These are ideas that we have found to be effective in teaching children to write different styles of text and tackling the common difficulties that tend to crop up during teaching.

🦖 Text-specific overviews

These overviews are separated into the following areas: text-specific features (e.g. a headline is a feature of a newspaper article) and the grammar, punctuation and spelling opportunities that you may expect to cover for that text type.

Text-specific features

These could be considered to be the 'building blocks' for writing different text types. For example, persuasive texts will include features like flattery and emotive language, whereas a non-chronological report will contain subheadings and factual statements.

Grammar, punctuation and spelling lists

These are some key grammar, spelling and punctuation opportunities that come up in the model texts. Under many of the points are example words, phrases or sentences.

Checklists

Each overview page ends with a checklist which teachers and children can use alongside the model texts. These can be used as a handy guide to aid planning and to support children's writing. The checklists highlight the features contained in the model texts and can be used for self, peer or teacher assessment.

These checklists are guides and not exhaustive lists. The model texts include many other grammar, spelling and punctuation opportunities, which are not listed in the checklists, and these can be taught where you think it is appropriate.

🦖 Model texts

Each model text has been written to meet the 'expected standard' or 'greater depth standard' for Key Stage 2 pupils. To make the features of the model text clear to you, we have included two versions:

1. Unannotated: these can be photocopied for pupils or displayed on a whiteboard or projector.
2. Annotated: the text-specific features and grammar, punctuation and spelling opportunities are all clearly detailed in this version.

You can use the model texts in a variety of ways. You can read them as examples of the expected standards for each year group and explore the different features present in each text. You can share the texts with your pupils, perhaps inviting them to annotate the texts themselves. You could even share the annotated texts with children to help them evaluate the writing.

Topic coverage

Grammarsaurus Key Stage 2 and its companion book for Key Stage 1 cover a wide range of topics, including history, geography and science. Here is an overview of the topic coverage for both books. This book is for Key Stage 2 only.

	Instructional texts	Explanation texts	Non-chronological reports	Recounts: diary entries	Recounts: newspaper articles	Persuasive texts
Year 1	How to prepare for a teddy bears' picnic	How is bread made?	Arctic animals	School trip to the seaside	*Not appropriate for Year 1 level*	Jack's magic beans
Year 2	How to find buried treasure	How do plants grow?	Marine mammals	A pirate's life	London's Burning!	T-Rex in town
Year 2 greater depth	How to build a castle	How do food chains work?	Kings and queens	Antarctic adventures	Gunpowder, Treason and Capture!	Adopt a wild animal!
Year 3	How to make a wizard's spell	How do shadow puppets work?	Roman soldiers	Queen Boudicca	Man Walks on the Moon!	Marvellous Mike's travelling circus
Year 4	How to survive an earthquake	How does the water cycle work?	The Titanic	Viking raider	Peril in Pompeii!	Ascend the astral throne!
Year 5	How to prepare for an intergalactic mission	How do volcanoes erupt?	Ancient Greek myths: the cyclops	The discovery of Tutankhamun's tomb	Marathon Man Brings News of Victory!	Join the Stellar Dome Community today!
Year 6	How to survive a zombie attack	How does blood circulate around the body?	The ancient Maya	Darwin's diary: The Galápagos Islands	Normandy Invaded!	Join the Women's Land Army
Year 6 greater depth	How to survive on a desert island	How does the internet work?	The Shang Dynasty	The mystery of the Mary Celeste	Heir to the Montagues Gatecrashes Ball	Visit the Great Exhibition

Useful words for Key Stage 2

The National Curriculum in England includes 'word lists' for Years 3 and 4 and Years 5 and 6. We have included these below. Whenever these words appear in the model texts, we have highlighted them, so you can quickly see which words are key spellings for children to learn.

Years 3 and 4

accident(ally)	famous	peculiar
actual(ly)	favourite	perhaps
address	February	popular
answer	forward(s)	position
appear	fruit	possess(ion)
arrive	grammar	possible
believe	group	potatoes
bicycle	guard	pressure
breath	guide	probably
breathe	heard	promise
build	heart	purpose
busy/business	height	quarter
calendar	history	question
caught	imagine	recent
centre	increase	regular
century	important	reign
certain	interest	remember
circle	island	sentence
complete	knowledge	separate
consider	learn	special
continue	length	straight
decide	library	strange
describe	material	strength
different	medicine	suppose
difficult	mention	surprise
disappear	minute	therefore
early	natural	though/although
earth	naughty	thought
eight/eighth	notice	through
enough	occasion(ally)	various
exercise	often	weight
experience	opposite	woman/women
experiment	ordinary	
extreme	particular	

Years 5 and 6

accommodate	disastrous	opportunity
accompany	embarrass	parliament
according	environment	persuade
achieve	equip (–ped, –ment)	physical
aggressive	especially	prejudice
amateur	exaggerate	privilege
ancient	excellent	profession
apparent	existence	programme
appreciate	explanation	pronunciation
attached	familiar	queue
available	foreign	recognise
average	forty	recommend
awkward	frequently	relevant
bargain	government	restaurant
bruise	guarantee	rhyme
category	harass	rhythm
cemetery	hindrance	sacrifice
committee	identity	secretary
communicate	immediate(ly)	shoulder
community	individual	signature
competition	interfere	sincere(ly)
conscience	interrupt	soldier
conscious	language	stomach
controversy	leisure	sufficient
convenience	lightning	suggest
correspond	marvellous	symbol
criticise (critic + ise)	mischievous	system
curiosity	muscle	temperature
definite	necessary	thorough
desperate	neighbour	twelfth
determined	nuisance	variety
develop	occupy	vegetable
dictionary	occur	vehicle
		yacht

CHAPTER 1

Instructional texts

The purpose of an instructional text is to help the reader learn something by providing a step-by-step guide.

Tips for teaching children to write instructional texts

🐾 Less confident writers can find it easier to write about things they have experience of. Consider inviting them to write about a simple recipe like making a sandwich or allowing them to create something crafty, which they can then write about.

🐾 Consider different ways children could plan their writing. After naming each section of the text, e.g. method, equipment list and introduction, plan and write each section separately in boxes to make the process easier.

🐾 To scaffold less confident writers, take photographs of the children as they complete a task and display them so that they have a visual reminder of what they did at each step, to use while they write.

🐾 To support children to write in chronological order, choose a topic and provide children with the steps involved on separate pieces of card. Ask children to place the steps in the correct order. Discuss how the use of more detailed time adverbials can make it easier to see which step goes where and encourage children to use time adverbials in their own writing. For example, instead of writing 'Once finished', children might write something more detailed such as 'Once the decoration on top of the cake has been completed...'

Teach a range of adverbials of time, including adverbial clauses, to add variety when children are writing a method. Otherwise, they may overuse 'next' and 'then'.

- **Following that**
- **When you have finished _____**
- **Once the _____ starts to _____**
- **Once _____ has been completed**
- **After _____ minutes**

Create an anchor chart (a visual prompt that provides children with information) with a range of examples of quantifiers to encourage the children to vary their expanded noun phrases.

- **several**
- **three spoonfuls of**
- **a slither of**
- **two handfuls of**
- **a selection of**
- **a large variety of**

Spend time focusing on how to spell words ending in -ful! These words are abundant in instructions and children sometimes spell these words with two 'l's and a space, for example, 'hand full' instead of 'handful'.

'Working at greater depth' explained

There are two texts for Year 6 level in this chapter. The second Year 6 text on pages 36 – 39 is designed to show 'greater depth'.

- The audience of the explanation text is clear throughout the piece of writing. The instructions are aimed at someone who is unaccustomed to survival skills and therefore precise, additional information is provided, e.g. 'Remember that the wood must be dry or the fire will not start when you attempt to light it with the lighter or flint.'

- The writing moves between an informal tone and a formal tone. In the introduction, hyperbole ('facing certain death') and a direct address to the reader using 'you' establishes an informal tone. In the numbered steps, there is a more formal, factual tone, with modal verbs frequently used in the passive voice ('food must be found'). By using an agentless passive, the sentence is more formal.

- More complicated vocabulary has been used, for example, 'sourced' instead of 'found', 'established' rather than 'lit' and 'constructed' instead of 'built'.

- Technical vocabulary is used, with words including 'foliage', 'sub-zero', 'firewood' and 'predators'.

- Higher-level punctuation is used, such as semi-colons.

Year 3 overview

Use this overview and the checklist alongside the Year 3 model text (pages 14 – 17).

🐾 Specific features for this text type

• A title statement explaining what is to be achieved	*How to make a Victoria sponge cake*
• A list of equipment or materials	*You will need the following ingredients.*
• Sequenced, chronological steps	
• Diagrams or illustrations	
• Present tense	*It is important to follow the steps in the correct order.*
• Imperative verbs (commands)	*Spread the cream...*
• Detailed information – prepositions, quantifiers and precise vocabulary	*Dust the top of the cake with icing sugar.*

The following lists should be used as a tool to help teachers plan where to cover explicit grammar, punctuation and spelling objectives from both the Teacher Assessment Framework and the National Curriculum Programmes of Study.

🐾 Grammar

• Coordinating conjunctions – link ideas with 'and', 'but' or 'or'	*Divide the mixture into two tins and place them in the oven.*
• Subordinating conjunctions – expand upon independent clauses using 'after', 'if', 'when', 'until' or 'so that'	*Mix the ingredients until you have a smooth, soft batter.*
• Expanded noun phrases – add detail to nouns using prepositions such as 'of', 'from', 'under', 'around', 'surrounding', 'next to' and 'above'	*the top of the cake*
• Commands, using the imperative	*Bake the cake for about 20 minutes.*
• Statements using the pronoun 'you'	*You will need...*
• Adverbs / adverbials of manner	*Carefully, sprinkle the icing sugar on top of the cake.*
• Adverbs / adverbials of time	*After 20 minutes...*

🐾 Punctuation

- Commas in a list   *a spatula, spoon and mixing bowl*
- Apostrophes for possession   *the cake's base*
- Apostrophes for omission   *Don't forget to...*

🐾 Spelling

- Year 3 / 4 words from the National Curriculum word lists: see page 9 of this book for a list of these. These words are highlighted in the Year 3 model text.
- Words ending in -ly   *slowly, carefully, quickly*
- Words ending in -ful   *spoonful, handful, jarful*

🐾 Checklist

Use this checklist with the Year 3 model text. See page 7 for more information.

Title statement	
List of equipment or materials	
Sequenced, chronological steps	
Diagrams or illustrations	
Present tense	
Imperative verbs (commands)	
Detailed information	
Grammar: Coordinating conjunctions	
Grammar: Subordinating conjunctions	
Grammar: Expanded noun phrases	
Grammar: Commands, using the imperative	
Grammar: Statements using the pronoun 'you'	
Grammar: Adverbs / adverbials of manner / time	
Punctuation: Commas in a list	
Punctuation: Apostrophes for possession	
Punctuation: Apostrophes for omission	
Spelling: Year 3 / 4 word list	
Spelling: Words ending in -ly	
Spelling: Words ending in -ful	

Year 3 model text

How to make a wizard's spell

Are you new to the fearful world of witchcraft and wizardry? If so, you may be struggling with spell-making. Fear not! Just think of a spell like a recipe!

Equipment

- a large, metal cauldron
- a mixing spoon
- a measuring jug
- a small flask
- a metal sieve
- a sharp knife
- a frying pan
- a dictionary of magical words

Ingredients

- a handful of frogs' legs
- a cat's whisker
- ten toenails from an ugly, smelly giant
- the peeled skin of 20 rotten potatoes
- a jarful of spit from a young boy or girl
- a spoonful of extra hot chilli sauce

Method

1. Firstly, collect the ingredients from your wizard's cupboard. If you do not own a cauldron, use a large mixing bowl.

2. Next, thoroughly mix together the chilli sauce, the toenails and three-quarters of the jar of spit so that you create a lumpy paste.

3. Following that, use the sieve to strain the liquid and separate the toenails from the potion or skip this step if you would prefer your potion to have extra crunch!

4. While the liquid is being strained, cautiously peel the rotten potatoes, but don't take too long. Add these to the mixture.

5. The frogs' legs and the cat's whisker must be fried for an hour until they are crispy. Gently combine these with the rest of the gruesome mixture.

7. Now, refer to the dictionary of magical words to find the correct chant for your spell and combine this with a downwards wand movement.

Congratulations! You have now successfully cast your first spell!

6. After allowing the potion to stew for three days, transfer it to a small flask.

Don't forget!

Magical spells can be extremely dangerous! You can't increase the quantities of the ingredients or your spell might backfire and you'll become seriously injured!

Chapter 1:
Instructional texts

Year 3 model text: annotated

Dark grey highlights = Words from the National Curriculum word lists

↓ title

How to make a wizard's spell

↓ word ending in -ful
Are you new to the fearful world of witchcraft and wizardry? If so, you may be
↑ question using the pronoun 'you'   subordinating conjunction ↑
struggling with spell-making. Fear not! Just think of a spell like a recipe!

Equipment
↓↑ list of equipment
- a large, metal cauldron
  ↑ comma for list
- a mixing spoon
- a measuring jug
- a small flask
- a metal sieve
- a sharp knife
- a frying pan
- a dictionary of magical words

Ingredients
- a handful of frogs' legs
  ↑ word ending in -ful
- a cat's whisker
- ten toenails from an
  ↑ expanded noun phrase using quantifier
  ugly, smelly giant
- the peeled skin of
  20 rotten potatoes
- a jarful of spit from
  ↑ expanded noun phrase using quantifier
  a young boy or girl
- a spoonful of extra hot chilli sauce
  ↑ word ending in -ful

Method
↓↑ sequenced steps
1. Firstly, collect the ingredients from your
   ↑ word ending in -ly
   wizard's cupboard. If you do not own
   a cauldron, use a large mixing bowl.
   ↑ expanded noun phrase

↓↑ sequenced steps   ↓ imperative
2. Next, thoroughly mix together the
   ↑ adverb of time   ↖ word ending in -ly
   chilli sauce, the toenails and three-
   ↑ comma for list
   quarters of the jar of spit so that you
   ↑ subordinating conjunction
   create a lumpy paste.

↓↑ sequenced steps
3. Following that, use the sieve to strain
   ↑ adverbial of time
   the liquid and separate the toenails
   ↑ coordinating conjunction
   from the potion or skip this step if you
   ↑ coordinating conjunction
   would prefer your potion to have
   extra crunch!

HOT SAUCE

↓↑ **sequenced steps**
4. While the liquid is being strained,

<u>cautiously</u> peel the rotten potatoes,
↑ **adverb of manner**
<u>but</u> don't take too long. Add these
↑ **coordinating conjunction**   ↑ **command**
to the mixture.

↓↑ **sequenced steps**
5. The frogs' legs and the cat's
↑↓ **apostrophes for possession**
whisker <u>must</u> be fried for an hour
↓→ **present tense** ────────────→
until they are crispy. <u>Gently</u> combine
↓→ **present tense** ──────→ ↑ **adverb of manner**
these with the rest of the gruesome

mixture.

↓↑ **sequenced steps**
7. Now, refer to <u>the dictionary of</u>
expanded noun phrase ↗
<u>magical words</u> to find the correct
↖ **expanded noun phrase**
chant for your spell and combine
present tense ↑↓→ ─────→
this with a downwards wand
↓→ **present tense** ──────────→
movement.
↑ **present tense**

Congratulations! You have now
↑ **statement using the pronoun 'you'**
successfully cast your first spell!

↓↑ **sequenced steps**
6. After allowing the potion to stew

for three days, transfer it to a

small flask.

Don't forget!
↑ **apostrophe for omission**
Magical spells can be

extremely dangerous! You
↑ **word ending in -ly**
can't increase **the quantities**
↑ **apostrophe for omission**
of the ingredients or your

spell might backfire <u>and</u> **you'll**
coordinating conjunction ↑
become seriously injured!

Year 4 overview

Use this overview and the checklist alongside the Year 4 model text (pages 20 – 23).

🐾 Specific features for this text type

• A title statement	*How to escape a dragon's lair*
• A list of equipment or materials	*Various pieces of equipment are needed...*
• Sequenced, chronological steps	
• Diagrams or illustrations	
• Present tense	*search, tie, hide, tiptoe*
• Imperative verbs (commands)	*Tiptoe towards the cavern.*
• Detailed information – prepositions, quantifiers and precise vocabulary	*Avoid any smoke-filled rooms.*

The following lists should be used as a tool to help teachers plan where to cover explicit grammar, punctuation and spelling objectives from both the Teacher Assessment Framework and the National Curriculum Programmes of Study.

🐾 Grammar

• Coordinating conjunctions – 'and', 'or' or 'but'	*Place the weapons in the cart and ensure...*
• Subordinating conjunctions – 'after', 'if', 'when' or 'so that'	*When the dragon is sleeping...*
• Expanded noun phrases – add detail to nouns using prepositions such as 'of' and 'from'	*the mouth of the dragon*
• Commands, using the imperative	*Follow the passageway.*
• Statements using the pronoun 'you'	*This guide requires you to...*
• Adverbs / adverbials of manner	*With the utmost care, tiptoe past...*
• Adverbs / adverbials of time	*for an hour*

🐾 Punctuation

• Commas in a list	*swords, shields and helmets*
• Commas for fronted adverbials	*When the dragon is asleep, you can enter the cave.*

- Apostrophes for possession   *the dragon's tail*
- Apostrophes for omission   *Don't touch the...*

🐾 Spelling

- Year 3 / 4 words from the National Curriculum word lists: see page 9 of this book for a list of these. These words are highlighted in the Year 4 model text.
- Words ending in -ly   *thoroughly, gradually, directly*
- Words ending in -ful   *boxful, bagful, spoonful*
- Words ending in -tion   *caution, position, section, protection, solution*

🐾 Checklist

Use this checklist with the Year 4 model text. See page 7 for more information.

Title statement	
List of equipment or materials	
Sequenced, chronological steps	
Diagrams or illustrations	
Present tense	
Imperative verbs (commands)	
Detailed information	
Grammar: Coordinating conjunctions	
Grammar: Subordinating conjunctions	
Grammar: Expanded noun phrases	
Grammar: Commands, using the imperative	
Grammar: Statements using the pronoun 'you'	
Grammar: Adverbs / adverbials of manner / time	
Punctuation: Commas in a list	
Punctuation: Commas for fronted adverbials	
Punctuation: Apostrophes for possession / omission	
Spelling: Year 3 / 4 word list	
Spelling: Words ending in -ly	
Spelling: Words ending in -ful	
Spelling: Words ending in -tion	

Year 4 model text

How to survive an earthquake

Is the ground shaking beneath your feet? Are you worried that an earthquake is about to strike?

These destructive natural disasters can strike without warning! You may have heard the famous phrase, 'Drop, cover and hold on,' but there is more to remember if you want to survive. Read on to find out more.

Instructions

1. As soon as you think that an earthquake is taking place, quickly drop to your hands and knees and crawl under a sturdy table or find a secure desk to hide underneath. These objects will provide protection from falling objects so that you are not injured.

Equipment

- a cushion, pillow or blanket
- thick-soled shoes
- a supply kit

Remember!
Don't stand in a doorway because it isn't as safe.

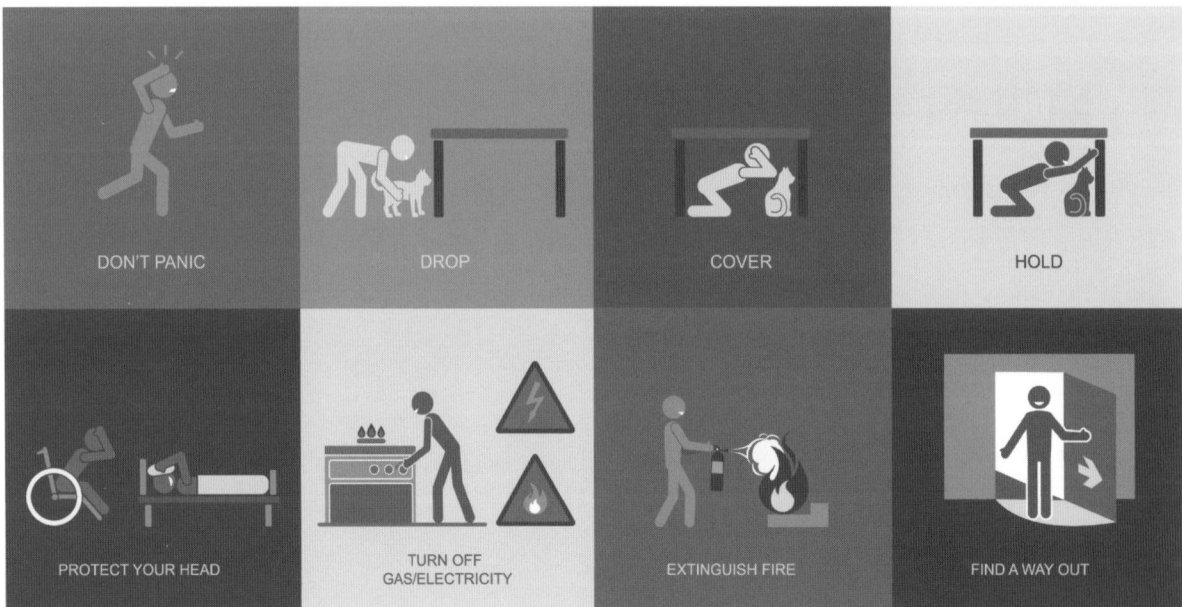

DON'T PANIC | DROP | COVER | HOLD

PROTECT YOUR HEAD | TURN OFF GAS/ELECTRICITY | EXTINGUISH FIRE | FIND A WAY OUT

2. When looking for somewhere to hide, move cautiously to avoid broken glass, large pieces of furniture or any other hazards, if you are able to.

3. After you have found somewhere to hide, protect your head and neck from falling debris which may be harmful. A cushion from the sofa, a pillow or a blanket can be used for this. If there is nothing nearby, use your hands and arms.

4. Do not move from your position for one to two minutes after the shaking has stopped. When you feel it is safe to move, carefully move from your safe location, but remain vigilant as the earthquake's aftershocks can be just as strong as the main earthquake.

5. Finally, cautiously move around after leaving your shelter and watch out for broken glass, debris and rubble around your home. If you aren't wearing shoes, move around with great care so that you don't injure your feet. Put on thick-soled shoes as quickly as possible as these will be useful to protect your feet.

Remember!

Being prepared is extremely important! You and your family should make a supply kit, devise an emergency plan and regularly practise these drills.

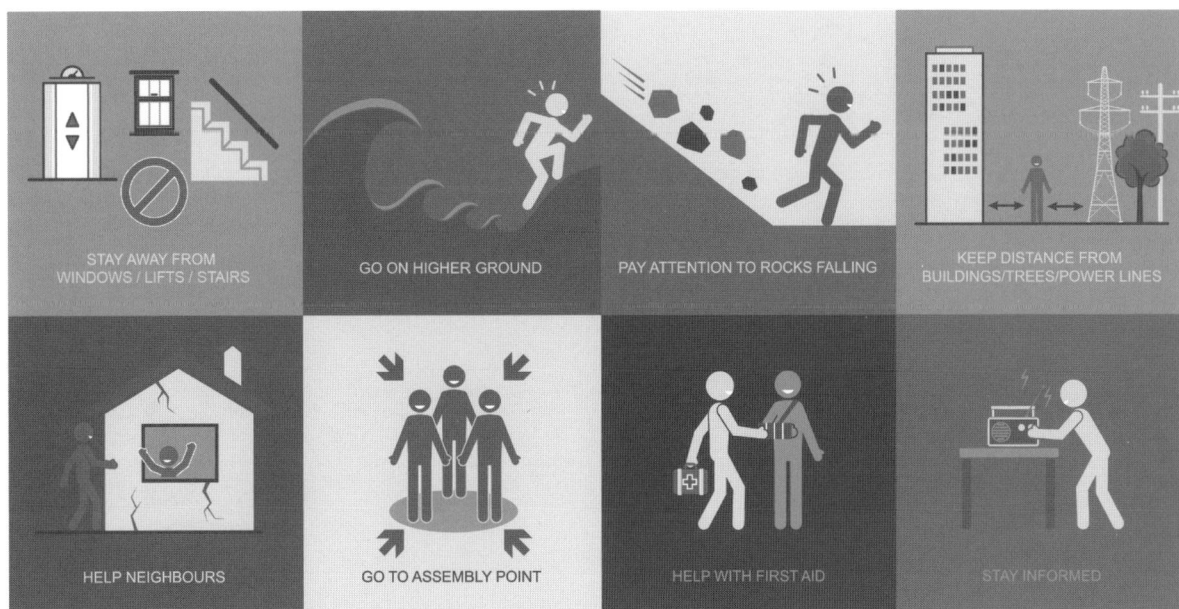

STAY AWAY FROM WINDOWS / LIFTS / STAIRS

GO ON HIGHER GROUND

PAY ATTENTION TO ROCKS FALLING

KEEP DISTANCE FROM BUILDINGS/TREES/POWER LINES

HELP NEIGHBOURS

GO TO ASSEMBLY POINT

HELP WITH FIRST AID

STAY INFORMED

Year 4 model text: annotated

Dark grey highlights = Words from the National Curriculum word lists

How to survive an earthquake
↑ title ─────────────────────────────────→

Is the ground shaking beneath your feet? Are you worried that an earthquake is about to strike?

↓↑ statement in the present tense
These destructive natural disasters can strike without warning! You may
↗ statements using the pronoun 'you'
have heard the famous phrase, 'Drop,
↖ statements using the pronoun 'you'
cover and hold on,' but there is more to
↑ coordinating conjunction
remember if you want to survive. Read
command ↗
on to find out more.
↖ command ─────→

Instructions
↓↑ sequenced steps
1. As soon as you think that an
earthquake is taking place, quickly
word ending in -ly ↑
drop to your hands and knees and
imperative ↗
crawl under a sturdy table or find a
↖ imperative   coordinating conjunction ↑
secure desk to hide underneath.

These objects will provide protection
word ending in -tion ↑
from falling objects so that you are
↑ subordinating conjunction
not injured.

Equipment
↓↑ list of equipment
- a cushion, pillow or blanket
- thick-soled shoes
↑ detailed information
- a supply kit

Remember!
Don't stand in a doorway

because it isn't as safe.
apostrophe for omission ↑

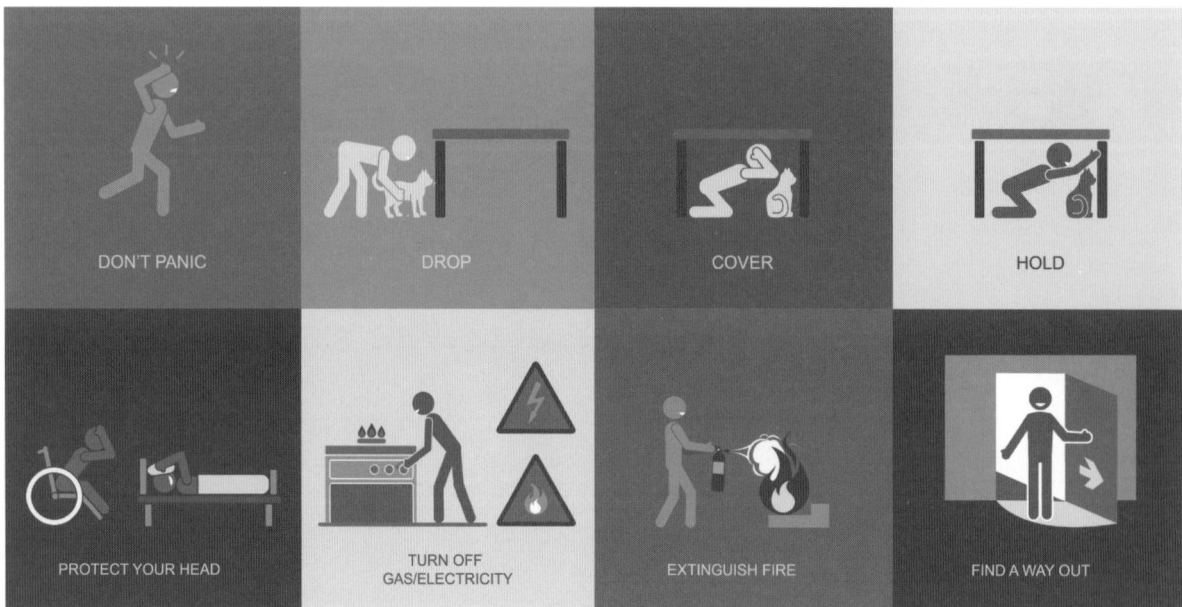

DON'T PANIC   DROP   COVER   HOLD

PROTECT YOUR HEAD   TURN OFF GAS/ELECTRICITY   EXTINGUISH FIRE   FIND A WAY OUT

Grammarsaurus KS2© Mitch Hudson and Anna Richards 2021

↓↑ sequenced steps

2. When looking for somewhere to hide,
↑ adverbial of time
move cautiously to avoid broken glass,
comma for list ↑
large pieces of furniture or any other

hazards, if you are able to.

↓↑ sequenced steps   comma for fronted adverbial ↓

3. After you have found somewhere to hide,
↑ subordinating conjunction
protect your head and neck from falling
word ending in -ful ↓
debris which may be harmful. A cushion
comma for list ↓   expanded noun phrase ↗
from the sofa, a pillow or a blanket
↖ expanded noun phrase
can be used for this. If there is nothing

nearby, use your hands and arms.

↓↑ sequenced steps

4. Do not move from your position for

one to two minutes after the shaking

has stopped. When you feel it is safe
↑ subordinating conjunction
to move, carefully move from your safe
↑ adverb of manner
location, but remain vigilant as the
↑ word ending in -tion
earthquake's aftershocks can be just as
↑ apostrophe for possession
strong as the main earthquake.

↓↑ sequenced steps

5. Finally, cautiously move around after
↑ adverb of time   ↖ adverb of manner
leaving your shelter and watch out

for broken glass, debris and rubble

around your home. If you aren't

wearing shoes, move around with
↑ comma for fronted adverbial
great care so that you don't injure

your feet. Put on thick-soled shoes as

quickly as possible as these will be

useful to protect your feet.
↑ word ending in -ful

Remember!

Being prepared is extremely
word ending in -ly ↑
important! You and your family

should make a supply kit, devise
comma for list ↑
an emergency plan and regularly
↑ expanded noun phrase   word ending in -ly ↑
practise these drills.

STAY AWAY FROM WINDOWS / LIFTS / STAIRS

GO ON HIGHER GROUND

PAY ATTENTION TO ROCKS FALLING

KEEP DISTANCE FROM BUILDINGS/TREES/POWER LINES

HELP NEIGHBOURS

GO TO ASSEMBLY POINT

HELP WITH FIRST AID

STAY INFORMED

Year 5 overview

Use this overview and the checklist alongside the Year 5 model text (pages 26 – 29).

🦕 Specific features for this text type

• A title statement explaining what is to be achieved	*How to attack an Anglo-Saxon settlement*
• A list of equipment or materials	*Your soldiers need the following weapons:*
• Sequenced, chronological steps	
• Diagrams or illustrations	
• Present tense	*attack, burn, destroy, invade, launch*
• Imperative verbs (commands)	*Launch the arrows…* *Raid the village…*
• Detailed information – prepositions, quantifiers and precise vocabulary	*several spearmen to defend the flanks*

The following lists should be used as a tool to help teachers plan where to cover explicit grammar, punctuation and spelling objectives from both the Teacher Assessment Framework and the National Curriculum Programmes of Study.

🦕 Grammar

• Coordinating conjunctions – link ideas with 'and', 'but' or 'or'	*Take control of the Great Hall and burn all the other buildings.*
• Subordinating conjunctions – expand upon independent clauses using 'after', 'if', 'when' or 'so that'	*If anyone tries to escape, make sure that you have additional men surrounding the settlement to stop them.*
• Expanded noun phrases – add detail to nouns using prepositions such as 'of', 'from', 'under', 'around', 'surrounding', 'next to' and 'above'	*the centre of the village* *the thatched roofs on top of each building*
• Commands, using the imperative	*Stash any gold that has been located.*
• Adverbs of manner	*Aggressively attack the enemy.*
• Adverbials of time	*in the depth of night* *just as the sun sets*

🐾 Punctuation

● Commas in a list	*archers, soldiers and horsemen*
● Parentheses	*...the thatched roofs – which are ideal for setting alight – can be targeted...*
● Apostrophes for possession	*the soldier's weapon*
● Commas for fronted adverbials	*After the cries of the villagers have finally ended, proceed to...*
● Colons	*You will need the following items:*

🐾 Spelling

● Year 5 / 6 words from the National Curriculum word lists: see page 9 of this book for a list of these. These words are highlighted in the Year 5 model text.

🐾 Checklist

Use this checklist with the Year 5 model text. See page 7 for more information.

Title statement	
List of equipment or materials	
Sequenced, chronological steps	
Diagrams or illustrations	
Present tense	
Imperative verbs (commands)	
Detailed information	
Grammar: Coordinating conjunctions	
Grammar: Subordinating conjunctions	
Grammar: Expanded noun phrases	
Grammar: Commands, using the imperative	
Grammar: Adverbs of manner	
Grammar: Adverbials of time	
Punctuation: Commas in a list	
Punctuation: Parentheses	
Punctuation: Apostrophes for possession	
Punctuation: Commas for fronted adverbials	
Punctuation: Colons	
Spelling: Year 5 / 6 word list	

Year 5 model text

How to prepare for an intergalactic mission

The moment has arrived – you have been selected by the world's top scientists!

Your intelligence, bravery and existing knowledge of alien lifeforms means you will be venturing into the depths of space in just a few months to save the planet from a potential invasion. How can you prepare yourself? Well, the greatest of minds have come together to write this handy guide for you! Follow these instructions carefully and save us all.

Our scientists are frequently asked about the existence of lifeforms on other planets. Up until now, we have been able to convince the world that this is not true, but the recent galactic invasion has awkwardly revealed to the world that we are not alone. Luckily for you, we know a thing or two about these creatures and so we have prepared a clear list of the equipment and personnel (humans to help) in your mission:

- A fully-equipped HUD-50-N spacecraft – this will be prepared for your mission, Captain!
- Soldiers to protect your crew
- Two highly-skilled cartographers

(mapping experts) to plot your journey, making sure to avoid crashing into asteroids
- Individual oxygen tanks for your comrades
- Several spacesuits with bio-temperature technology

Before you set off

1. Before you do anything else, scroll the secret, global space agency database to find the right soldiers to protect your crew. Aliens are aggressive beings, so weapons experts, especially those experienced in plasma and laser weaponry, will be necessary members of your crew if you are determined to survive this long journey.

2. Once you have hired the soldiers, find and interview skilled cartographers. At least two will be needed for your journey so that the spacecraft can avoid any dangerous celestial objects like meteorites and black holes. Time must be spent choosing the right

people for this role as the wrong turn in space could lead to certain death!

3. After all the personnel are trained and prepared, speak directly with the National Oxygen Factory (N.O.F.) to get oxygen tanks for the mission. Past space missions have been ended early due to a lack of oxygen, and it is necessary that you are successful in your venture!

4. Following that, arrange a meeting with our specialist laboratory technicians so that you and all your crew can be fitted into your spacesuits. Make sure that all your protective gear is strong against corrosive materials like acid – the vicious lifeforms you

will encounter have acidic saliva, so a bite from them will cause your suit to melt immediately. For this reason, instruct the technicians to attach jet packs to all suits so that your crew can make a speedy escape if they become surrounded by the extraterrestrial beings!

5. Finally, take the time to eat your favourite foods and spend time with family and friends before your mission! You are expected to be away for ten years and the packaged tubes of food in space are no match for a burger.

Good luck on your space adventure.

Professor Yukanov

Year 5 model text: annotated

Dark grey highlights = Words from the National Curriculum word lists

How to prepare for
↑↓ title
an intergalactic mission

The moment has arrived – you have been selected by the world's top scientists!

↑ apostrophe for possession

Your intelligence, bravery and existing

↑ comma for list

knowledge of alien lifeforms means you will be venturing into the depths of space in just a few months to save the planet from a potential invasion. How can you prepare yourself? Well, the greatest

expanded noun phrase ↗

of minds have come together to write

↖ expanded noun phrase

this handy guide for you! Follow these instructions carefully and save us all.

↑ adverb of manner

Our scientists are frequently asked about the existence of lifeforms on other planets. Up until now, we have been able to convince the world that this is not true, but the recent galactic invasion has awkwardly revealed to the world that we are not alone. Luckily for you, we know a thing or two about these creatures and so we have prepared a clear list of the equipment and personnel (humans to

parenthesis ↗

help) in your mission:

↖ parenthesis   ↑ colon

• A fully-equipped HUD-50-N spacecraft

↓↑ list of equipment

– this will be prepared for your mission, Captain!

• Soldiers to protect your crew

• Two highly-skilled cartographers

↓↑ list of equipment

(mapping experts) to plot your journey,

↑ parenthesis

making sure to avoid crashing into asteroids

• Individual oxygen tanks for your comrades

• Several spacesuits with bio-temperature technology

Before you set off

↓↑ sequenced steps

1. Before you do anything else, scroll the

comma for fronted adverbial ↑

secret, global space agency database to find the right soldiers to protect your crew. Aliens are aggressive beings, so weapons experts, especially those

↑ coordinating conjunction

experienced in plasma and laser

coordinating conjunction ↑

weaponry, will be necessary members of your crew if you are determined to survive this long journey.

↓↑ sequenced steps

2. Once you have hired the soldiers, find

↑ adverbial of time   imperative ↗

and interview skilled cartographers.

↖ imperative

At least two will be needed for your journey so that the spacecraft can avoid any dangerous celestial objects like meteorites and black holes. Time

present tense ↗

must be spent choosing the right

present tense ↗

↓↑ **sequenced steps**
people for this role as the wrong turn in
↖ **present tense**
space could lead to certain death!

↓↑ **sequenced steps**
3. After all the personnel are trained
↓ **adverb of manner**
and prepared, speak directly with
↑ **comma for fronted adverbial**
the National Oxygen Factory (N.O.F.)
parenthesis ↑
to get oxygen tanks for the mission.

Past space missions have been ended

early due to a lack of oxygen, and it
coordinating conjunction ↑
is necessary that you are successful in

your venture!

↓↑ **sequenced steps**
4. Following that, arrange a meeting with
↑ **adverbial of time**
our specialist laboratory technicians

so that you and all your crew can be
↑ **subordinating conjunction**   ↓→ **command** →
fitted into your spacesuits. Make
↓→ **command** ———————
sure that all your protective gear is
↓→ **command** ———————
strong against corrosive materials
↓ **command**
like acid – the vicious lifeforms you
↑ **expanded noun phrase**

↓↑ **sequenced steps**
will encounter have acidic saliva,

so a bite from them will cause your
↑ **coordinating conjunction**
suit to melt immediately. For this

reason, instruct the technicians to

attach jet packs to all suits so that

your crew can make a speedy escape

if they become surrounded by the

extraterrestrial beings!

↓↑ **sequenced steps**
5. Finally, take the time to eat your

favourite foods and spend time with

family and friends before your mission!

You are expected to be away for ten
detailed information ↗
years and the packaged tubes of food
↖ **detailed information**   **expanded noun phrase** ↗
in space are no match for a burger.
↖ **expanded noun phrase**

Good luck on your space adventure.

Professor Yukanov

Year 6 overview

Use this overview and the checklist alongside the Year 6 model texts (pages 32 – 39).

🦕 Specific features for this text type

● A title statement	*How to survive an alien invasion*
● A list of equipment or materials	*The following equipment is essential for survival:*
● Sequenced, chronological steps	
● Diagrams or illustrations	
● Present tense	*prepare, launch, locate, identify*
● Imperative verbs (commands)	*Prepare the aerial defence system.*
● Detailed information – prepositions, quantifiers and precise vocabulary	*Plot a course along the celestial highway.*

The following lists should be used as a tool to help teachers plan where to cover explicit grammar, punctuation and spelling objectives from both the Teacher Assessment Framework and the National Curriculum Programmes of Study.

🦕 Grammar

● Coordinating conjunctions – link ideas with 'and', 'but' or 'or'	*Assign your aerial fleet or ground forces to the most qualified general.*
● Subordinating conjunctions – 'after', 'if', 'when' or 'so that'	*If the first counterattack fails, be prepared for a secondary wave.*
● Expanded noun phrases – add detail to nouns using prepositions such as 'of', 'from', 'under', 'around', 'surrounding', 'next to' and 'above'	*the shields surrounding the capital ships* *the force field above planet Earth*
● Commands, using the imperative	*Barrage the enemy ships.*
● Adverbs of manner	*Carefully plan...* *Strategically link...*
● Adverbials of time	*as the enemy fleet approaches*

🦕 Punctuation

● Commas in a list	*plasma weaponry, anti-ship gunners and radar command*

Grammarsaurus KS2© Mitch Hudson and Anna Richards 2021

• Parentheses	*Our ships, which have been designed to repel all alien energy weaponry, are...*
• Apostrophes for possession	*the ship's motion sensor*
• Apostrophes for omission	*The aliens haven't got a chance.*
• Commas for fronted adverbials	*When the enemy draws closer, immediately fire...*
• Colons	*Your squadrons require the following reinforcing equipment:*

🐾 Spelling

- Year 5 / 6 words from the National Curriculum word lists: see page 9 of this book for a list of these. These words are highlighted in the Year 6 model texts.

🐾 Checklist

Use this checklist with the Year 6 model text. See page 7 for more information.

Title statement	
List of equipment or materials	
Sequenced, chronological steps	
Diagrams or illustrations	
Present tense	
Imperative verbs (commands)	
Detailed information	
Grammar: Coordinating conjunctions	
Grammar: Subordinating conjunctions	
Grammar: Expanded noun phrases	
Grammar: Commands, using the imperative	
Grammar: Adverbs of manner	
Grammar: Adverbials of time	
Punctuation: Commas in a list	
Punctuation: Parentheses	
Punctuation: Apostrophes for possession	
Punctuation: Apostrophes for omission	
Punctuation: Commas for fronted adverbials	
Punctuation: Colons	
Spelling: Year 5 / 6 word list	

Year 6 model text 1

How to survive a zombie attack

Imagine this - you're sat eating your dinner on a Thursday night and all of a sudden you hear a loud groan... Gran isn't visiting. The dog's sleeping soundly at your feet. So, what else could it be? You get up to pull back the curtains, and there before your eyes is a rotting corpse, licking its lips, ready for its own dinner. There can only be one explanation: a zombie outbreak! So, what do you do?

Equipment

Fortunately, with the world coming to an end and no police on the streets, it will be easy to take any of the following equipment from your local, trashed supermarkets or the back gardens of your fleeing neighbours:

- Anything strong enough to knock off a zombie's head – a cricket bat is perfect for this
- Multiple cans of tinned food
- A can opener – how else will you open the tins?

- Any kind of rope, including the skipping variety
- A trusty hammer and a good supply of nails
- Several planks of wood – head to the sawmill!

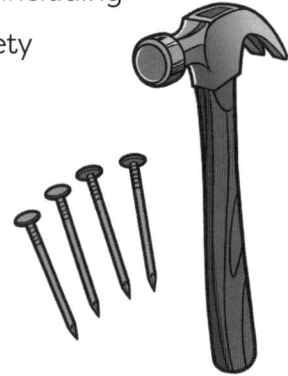

Method

1. After you have collected the necessary items above, find a building with very few ground-floor windows and plenty of stairs – a castle would be the perfect location if you see one nearby. You must remember that zombies are brain-dead creatures who struggle with opening doors and climbing stairs, so a spiral staircase up a tower will certainly have them stumbling and falling backwards.

2. If there are any ground-floor windows, simply use your planks of wood to nail them shut. It is a common fact that a zombie's fingers aren't as nimble as ours, so they'll struggle to remove the planks once nailed down.

3. When all possible window entries are covered, get to work on the main door to your building. At this point, you will have probably run out of wood, but that doesn't even matter! If you've watched any zombie film before, you'll notice that these ugly monsters are very slow and very dumb. Use this to your advantage and stretch and nail a simple rope across the bottom of your entranceway. In no time, the zombie horde entering your new home will trip, fall and never be able to get up again! Sorted!

4. Once your building is thoroughly secure, organise your human followers. They will now look to you as their saviour and leader. Enjoy this moment! It means you will never have to open any of the tins you swiped from the supermarket earlier that day. You just need to decide whether it's vegetable soup or beans for dinner.

5. Your cricket bat – or another strong weapon – is your new best friend. Sleep with it next to you in case the boarded windows, rope traps and staircases fail to stop zombies! If the worst comes to the worst, aim well and hit hard. A zombie's head is as fragile as a grape and will pop off into the distance with a decent swing of a bat.

If you were bitten during any of these steps, don't be afraid! Your future is simple – doomed! Enjoy your new life feasting on the brains of Mrs Hatherton at number 34.

Year 6 model text 1: annotated

Dark grey highlights = Words from the National Curriculum word lists

How to survive a zombie attack
↑ title

Imagine this - you're sat eating your
↑ apostrophe for omission

dinner on a Thursday night and all of a

sudden you hear a loud groan... Gran
↓ apostrophe for omission

isn't visiting. The dog's sleeping soundly
↑ apostrophe for omission

at your feet. So, what else could it be?

You get up to pull back the curtains,

and there before your eyes is a rotting

corpse, licking its lips, ready for its
detailed information ↗

own dinner. There can only be one
↖ detailed information

explanation: a zombie outbreak! So,

what do you do?

Equipment

Fortunately, with the world coming to

an end and no police on the streets,

it will be easy to take any of the

following equipment from your

local, trashed supermarkets
↓ coordinating conjunction

or the back gardens of your
expanded noun phrase ↗

fleeing neighbours:
↖ expanded noun phrase   ↑ colon

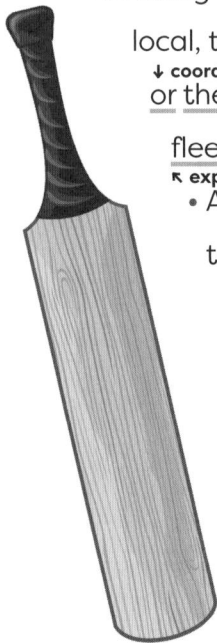

- Anything strong enough

  to knock off a zombie's

  head – a cricket bat is

  perfect for this

  - Multiple cans   ↙ expanded
                      noun phrase
  of tinned food   with quantifiers

  - A can opener – how

    else will you open

    the tins?

- Any kind of rope, including

  the skipping variety

- A trusty hammer

  and a good

  supply of nails

- Several planks

  of wood – head

  to the sawmill!

Method

1. After you have collected the necessary
   ↑ subordinating conjunction
   items above, find a building with
   comma for fronted adverbial ↑   expanded noun phrase ↗
   very few ground-floor windows and
                              expanded noun phrase ↗
   plenty of stairs – a castle would be
   ↖ expanded noun phrase
   the perfect location if you see one

   nearby. You must remember that

   zombies are brain-dead creatures

   who struggle with opening doors and

   climbing stairs, so a spiral staircase

   up a tower will certainly have them

   stumbling and falling backwards.

2. If there are any ground-floor windows,
   ↑ subordinating conjunction
   simply use your planks of wood to nail
   ↑ command
   them shut. It is a common fact that a

   zombie's fingers aren't as nimble as
   ↑ apostrophe for possession
   ours, so they'll struggle to remove the

   planks once nailed down.

3. <u>When</u> all possible window entries
↑ subordinating conjunction
are covered, get to work on the main

door to your building. At this point,

you will have probably run out of

wood, <u>but</u> that doesn't even matter!
↑ coordinating conjunction
If you've watched any zombie film

before, you'll notice that these ugly

monsters are very slow <u>and</u> very
coordinating conjunction ↑
dumb. <u>Use this to your advantage</u>
↑ imperative
and stretch and nail a simple

rope across the bottom of your

entranceway. In no time, the zombie

horde entering your new home will

trip, fall and never be able to get
↑ comma for list
up again! Sorted!

4. <u>Once your building is thoroughly</u>
↑ adverbial of time   ↑ adverb of manner
<u>secure,</u> organise your human followers.
↑ comma for fronted adverbial
They will now look to you as their

saviour and leader. Enjoy this

moment! It means you will never

have to open any of the tins you

swiped from the supermarket earlier

that day. You just need to decide

whether it's vegetable soup or

beans for dinner.

5. Your cricket bat – or another strong
↑ dashes for parenthesis
weapon – is your new best friend.

Sleep with it next to you in case the

boarded windows, rope traps and
↑ comma for list
staircases fail to stop zombies! If

the worst comes to the worst, aim

well and hit hard. A zombie's head
↓↑ detailed information →
is as fragile as a grape and will pop
↓↑ detailed information
off into the distance with a decent
↓↑ detailed information
swing of a bat.
↑ detailed information

If you were bitten during any of these

steps, don't be afraid! Your future is

simple – doomed! <u>Enjoy your new life</u>
↑ imperative
feasting on the brains of Mrs Hatherton

at number 34.

Year 6 model text 2

How to survive on a desert island

Lost! Abandoned! Alone! These are three words which you don't want to think about if you find yourself on an unfamiliar desert island, having just escaped the jaws of death.

One minute, you are sailing on your luxury yacht on a holiday of a lifetime. The next, you find yourself facing certain death shipwrecked on a desert island! If this sounds like your current predicament, then fear not: help is here!

Equipment list

Clearly, this is not a pre-planned event; therefore, the suggested equipment is a guide and it may be possible to scavenge similar items from the flotsam of the shipwreck:

- a sharp knife
- multiple pieces of rope or rope fashioned from bendable twigs and roots
- a bucket (or another piece of apparatus which can carry water effectively)
- dry logs, sticks and twigs
- a lighter or flint

Method

1. Initially, it is imperative for anyone who has found themself in a dangerous environment to give themself some time to think and collect their thoughts. After all, the Scouts, who are highly regarded in such matters, recommend the use of the mnemonic STOP: 'Stop, Think, Observe, Plan'. It is important to allow at least thirty minutes to complete this step if success

is to be guaranteed: it will provide the castaway with a chance to calm down and make sensible decisions.

2. At the earliest convenience, water – fresh water, not salt water from the sea – must be located as a priority. Without it, survival is unlikely! Cautiously, fill the bucket with the precious liquid and use a piece of material to filter the dirt from it; this will make it drinkable. (It is also possible to use a coconut to create a natural filter.)

3. Next, it is necessary to build a fire: this will provide vital heat, attract attention from passing ships and should deter wild predators – hopefully! Spend time retrieving firewood from the surrounding area for roughly an hour; this will ensure that sufficient wood has been collected for both the fire and the shelter. Remember that the wood must be dry or the fire will not start when you attempt to light it with the lighter or flint.

4. When the fire is well-established, a shelter must be carefully constructed. Use the wood which was collected earlier to create a simple structure. Rope, which is needed to secure the branches, can be made from thin and bendable branches. The leaves and foliage from the surrounding trees and bushes should be cut with a sharp knife; this will provide the cover needed to keep out the night's cold winds and sub-zero temperatures. However, take care to not exert too much energy on this task, especially if food has not yet been sourced.

5. Immediately after the shelter has been built, food must be found. It can be difficult to recognise the wide variety of edible fauna and flora when in the wild; however, if great care is taken, it is possible to find a whole plethora of food which will not lead to stomach upset.

A final note of warning. This guide has shown that, with some ingenuity and clever thinking, it's possible for you or anyone else – even the most biophobic of people – to sustain themselves in the wild using little more than what nature has provided. However, it is essential that steps are taken to protect yourself from predators which are likely to lurk in the undergrowth. If you don't do this, all of this will have been completed in vain!

Year 6 model text 2: annotated

Dark grey highlights = Words from the National Curriculum word lists

How to survive on a desert island
↑ title

Lost! Abandoned! Alone! These are three words which you don't want
↑ noun phrase with quantifier
to think about if you find yourself on an **unfamiliar** desert island,
having just escaped the jaws of death.

One minute, you are sailing on your
luxury yacht on a holiday of a lifetime.
↑ expanded noun phrase
The next, you find yourself facing certain
death shipwrecked on a desert island! If
this sounds like your current predicament,
then fear not: help is here!
colon ↑

Equipment list

Clearly, this is not a pre-planned event;
therefore, the suggested equipment is
a guide and it may be possible to
scavenge similar items from the flotsam
of the shipwreck:
↓↑ list of equipment
• a sharp knife
↓ expanded noun phrase with quantifier
• multiple pieces of rope or rope fashioned
detailed information ↗
from bendable twigs and roots
↖ detailed information

↓↑ list of equipment
• a bucket (or another piece of apparatus
parenthesis ↗
which can carry water effectively)
↖ parenthesis
• dry logs, sticks and twigs
↑ comma for list
• a lighter or flint

Method
↓↑ sequenced steps
1. Initially, it is imperative for anyone who
↑ adverb of time   ↖ present tense
has found themselves in a dangerous
environment to give themself
some time to think and collect their
thoughts. After all, the Scouts, who
are highly regarded in such matters,
recommend the use of the mnemonic
STOP: 'Stop, Think, Observe, Plan'. It
is important to allow at least thirty
minutes to complete this step if success
subordinating conjunction ↑

↓↑ sequenced steps

is to be guaranteed: it will provide the
colon ↑
castaway with a chance to calm down

and make sensible decisions.
↑ coordinating conjunction

↓↑ sequenced steps

↓ comma for fronted adverbial

2. At the earliest convenience, water –
parenthesis ↗
fresh water, not salt water from the sea
parenthesis ↗
– must be located as a priority. Without
↖ parenthesis
it, survival is unlikely! Cautiously, fill the
adverb of manner ↑
bucket with the precious liquid and

use a piece of material to filter the

dirt from it; this will make it drinkable.

(It is also possible to use a coconut to
parenthesis ↗
create a natural filter.)

↓↑ sequenced steps

3. Next, it is necessary to build a fire: this
↑ adverb of time   *colon ↑*
will provide vital heat, attract attention

from passing ships and should deter

wild predators – hopefully! Spend
↑ parenthesis
time retrieving firewood from the

surrounding area for roughly an hour;

this will ensure that sufficient wood has

been collected for both the fire and

the shelter. Remember that the wood

must be dry or the fire will not start
↑ coordinating conjunction
when you attempt to light it with the

lighter or flint.

↓↑ sequenced steps

comma for fronted adverbial ↓

4. When the fire is well-established, a
↑ subordinating conjunction
shelter must be carefully constructed.
adverb of manner ↑
Use the wood which was collected
↓↑ command
earlier to create a simple structure.
↓↑ command
Rope, which is needed to secure the

↓↑ sequenced steps

branches, can be made from thin and

bendable branches. The leaves and
expanded noun phrase ↗
foliage from the surrounding trees
expanded noun phrase ↗
and bushes should be cut with a sharp
↖ expanded noun phrase
knife; this will provide the cover needed

to keep out the night's cold winds and
↑ apostrophe for possession
sub-zero temperatures. However, take

care to not exert too much energy on

this task, especially if food has not yet

been sourced.

↓↑ sequenced steps

5. Immediately after the shelter has
↑ subordinating conjunction
been built, food must be found. It
↑ comma for fronted adverbial
can be difficult to recognise the wide

variety of edible fauna and flora when

in the wild; however, if great care is

taken, it is possible to find a whole

plethora of food which will not lead

to stomach upset.

A final note of warning. This guide has

shown that, with some ingenuity and

clever thinking, it's possible for you or
↑ apostrophe for omission
anyone else – even the most biophobic

of people – to sustain themselves in the

wild using little more than what nature

has provided. However, it is essential

that steps are taken to protect yourself

from predators which are likely to lurk

in the undergrowth. If you don't
apostrophe for omission ↑
do this, all of this will have been

completed in vain!

Explanation texts

The purpose of an explanation text is to explain to the reader how something works or why something happens.

Tips for teaching children to write explanation texts

🐾 Explanation texts and instructional texts can sometimes be confused. Remind children that explanation texts explain **why** something happens or **how** something works whilst instructional texts usually explain how to do something in a step-by-step guide. In terms of the audience, the reader of an instructional text is expected to follow the steps, whereas the reader of an explanation text is looking for general information about a process.

Ash cloud

Crater

Lava flow

Conduit (pipe)

Layers of ash

Layers of lava

Bedrock

Magma

🐾 It is often easier for children to write explanations about something fictional, such as a new invention. This can allow children to focus on the grammar, punctuation and spelling skills rather than getting lost in the details of a real-life topic.

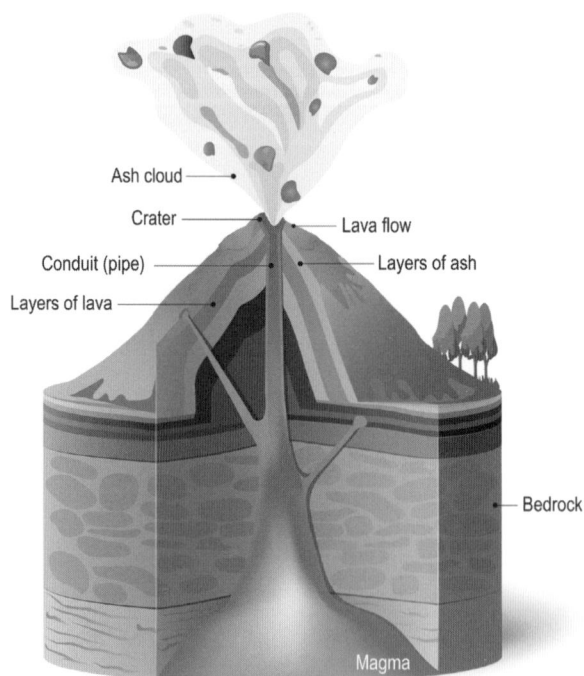

🐾 Show children different ways to plan an explanation text. Flow charts are useful as they remind children that each step should flow on to the next. A flow chart could be constructed together as a class, for example, on a whiteboard. Use arrows to link the different stages of the text. To support further, you might ask the children to record the adverbials of time they will use and write these on the whiteboard, between each stage.

🐾 In addition to or instead of flow charts, less confident writers could start by ordering pictures showing a process and then labelling each stage rather than writing a whole explanation text straight away.

🐾 Remind children that explanations must seem factual (even if the topic is about something fictional) and therefore, their language choices should be technical. Use different discussion-based activities before writing so that children are confident using the technical vocabulary associated with the topic. Activities might include identifying the different parts of a flower with a partner or placing event cards in the correct order and explaining how they decided on this order.

'Working at greater depth' explained

🐾 There are two texts for Year 6 level in this chapter. The second Year 6 text (pages 66 – 69) is designed to show 'greater depth'.

- The introduction and conclusion both address the reader directly, for example, 'your computer in Australia' and 'the next time someone sends you a photo'.

- The writing moves between an informal tone and a formal tone. In the introduction, exaggerated language is used, such as 'lightning speed' and there are references to familiar concepts such as computers 'speaking' to each other or sending holiday photos. After that, a more formal, factual tone is used, with verbs used in the passive voice ('the computers are connected'). By using an agentless passive, the sentence is more formal as it avoids determining who has connected the computers and makes the sentence more succinct.

- Higher-level punctuation is used, such as semi-colons.

- Technical vocabulary is used, with words including 'network', 'router', 'devices' and 'fibre optic cables'.

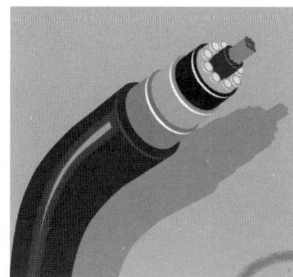

Year 3 overview

Use this overview and the checklist alongside the Year 3 model text (pages 44 – 47).

🦴 Specific features for this text type

• A clear title	*How do bees make honey?*
• An introductory paragraph – say what is going to be explained	*Many people are unaware of...*
• Paragraphs detailing a process, often in chronological order	
• Facts	*Bees have four wings.*
• Present tense	*The sugar is changed to energy.*
• Formal language	*This process is called pollination.*
• Technical vocabulary	*pollen, fertilisation, gestation*

The following lists should be used as a tool to help teachers plan where to cover explicit grammar, punctuation and spelling objectives from both the Teacher Assessment Framework and the National Curriculum Programmes of Study.

🦴 Grammar

• Coordinating conjunctions – link ideas with 'and', 'but', 'so' and 'for'	*Bees collect nectar so they can make honey.*
• Subordinating conjunctions – expand upon independent clauses with 'when', 'as', 'before', 'since' and 'although' / 'even though'	*When a bee collects pollen from the flower, some of it sticks to the hairs on its body.*
• Expanded noun phrases – add detail to nouns	*the sticky, sweet nectar*
• Adverbs / adverbials of time	*following that, soon after, moments later*
• Adverbs / adverbials of manner – say how something is done	*Buzzing rapidly, the bee creates vibrations to shake the plant's pollen.*

🦴 Punctuation

• Apostrophes for possession	*the bee's wings*
• Commas for lists	*Their bodies are yellow, black and fluffy.*

🐾 Spelling

- Year 3 / 4 words from the National Curriculum word lists: see page 9 of this book for a list of these. These words are highlighted in the Year 3 model text.
- Words ending in -ly   *slowly, carefully, quickly*

🐾 Checklist

Use this checklist with the Year 3 model text. See page 7 for more information.

Title	
Introductory paragraph	
Paragraphs detailing a process	
Facts	
Present tense	
Formal language	
Technical vocabulary	
Grammar: Coordinating conjunctions	
Grammar: Subordinating conjunctions	
Grammar: Expanded noun phrases	
Grammar: Adverbs / adverbials of time	
Grammar: Adverbs / adverbials of manner	
Punctuation: Apostrophes for possession	
Punctuation: Commas for lists	
Spelling: Year 3 / 4 word list	
Spelling: Words ending in -ly	

Year 3 model text

How do shadow puppets work?

Shadow puppetry (which can also be known as shadow play) is a very ancient and popular form of storytelling and has been used for many centuries as a form of entertainment around the world.

It is performed in various countries such as China, India, Nepal and Egypt. Shadow puppets actually rely on very simple science in order to work. Read on to find out how they work.

Before starting the show, a translucent screen or **scrim** is needed to cast the shadows onto and for the audience to watch the show on.

> *A **scrim** is a woven material. It can be either a finely-woven, lightweight fabric, often used in theatres, or it can be a heavy, woven material.*

After the screen has been constructed, the puppets are made. The material used for them can vary, although it must be something solid which will cast a dark shadow. The puppets are usually made out of card or plastic, but can also be made out of leather.

Once the basic shapes have been made, more detail is added so that the characters appear more interesting. Shapes are accurately cut away so features such as the eyes or eyebrows are represented. Additionally, colour can be added by inserting some coloured paper or gel for this will allow light to shine through the puppet and cast a coloured glow on the screen.

> *Did you know that a person's hands can also be used to create puppets? In fact, anything that will block part of the light travelling from the light source to the screen can be used!*

The creation of a shadow ↓

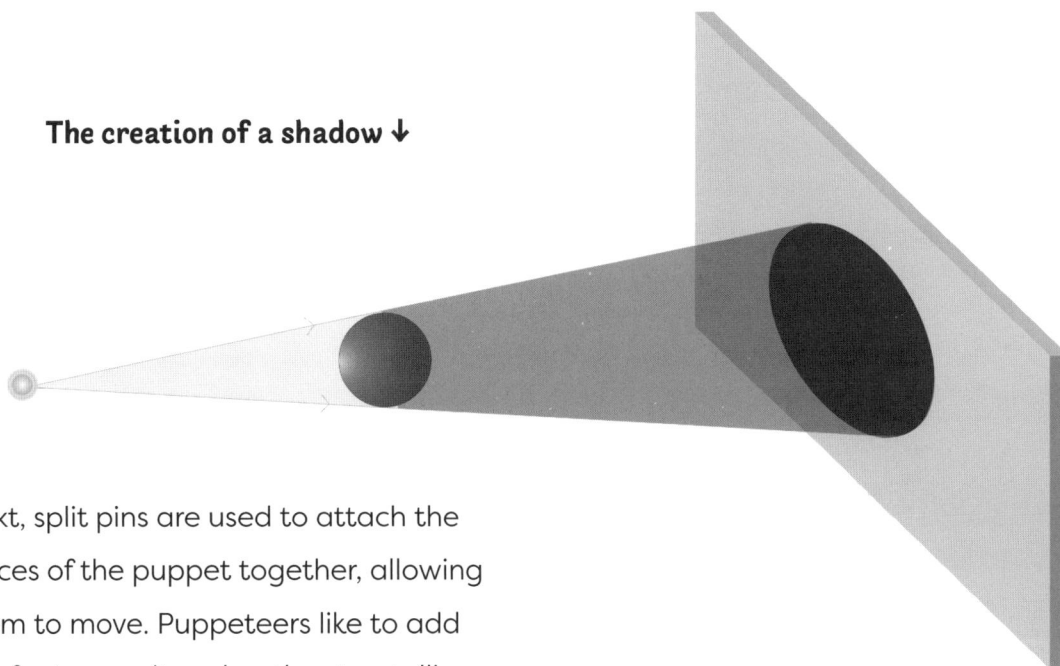

Next, split pins are used to attach the pieces of the puppet together, allowing them to move. Puppeteers like to add this feature as it makes the storytelling more interesting.

Following that, the light source needs to be created, since the show will not work without it! Any light source can be used, for example, a candle, a torch or a lantern. Light travels in a straight line and it will continue until it meets an opaque (solid) object. The puppet is placed between the lamp and the screen to create a shadow. When the light's rays are blocked, a shadow is made. Shadow puppeteers' knowledge of this science is used to successfully create their shows. Interestingly, the closer the puppet is to the light, the more light waves are blocked, so the bigger the shadow will be.

Finally, once the screen, puppets and light source are all ready, the show can begin. Moving the puppets behind the screen creates the illusion that the puppets are moving on their own. Very talented and experienced puppeteers can make the figures appear to walk, talk, fight and even dance.

When the light source is removed, by turning off the light, the shadows will disappear and the show is over!

Year 3 model text: annotated

Dark grey highlights = Words from the National Curriculum word lists

How do shadow puppets work?
↑ title

↓ introduction

Shadow puppetry (which can also be known as shadow play) is a very ancient

and popular form of storytelling and has been used for many centuries as
↑ coordinating conjunction

a form of entertainment around the world.

It is performed in various countries

such as China, India, Nepal and Egypt.
↑ commas for list

Shadow puppets actually rely on very
↑ word ending in -ly

simple science in order to work. Read on

to find out how they work.

↓ paragraphs detailing a process

Before starting the show, a translucent
technical vocabulary ↗

screen or **scrim** is needed to cast the
↖ technical vocabulary

shadows onto and for the audience to

watch the show on.

↓ technical vocabulary

*A **scrim** is a woven material.*

It can be either a finely-woven,

lightweight fabric, often used

in theatres, or it can be a heavy,
comma for list ↑

woven material.

↓↑ paragraphs detailing a process

Once the basic shapes have been
↑ expanded noun phrase

made, more detail is added so that the

characters appear more interesting.

Shapes are accurately cut away so
↖ word ending in -ly

features such as the eyes or eyebrows are

represented. Additionally, colour can be
↑ word ending in -ly

added by inserting some coloured paper

or gel for this will allow light to shine
↖ coordinating conjunction

through the puppet and cast a coloured

glow on the screen.

↓↑ paragraphs detailing a process

After the screen has been constructed,
↑ subordinating conjunction

the puppets are made. The material used

for them can vary, although it must be
subordinating conjunction ↑

something solid which will cast a dark

shadow. The puppets are usually made

out of card or plastic, but can also be

made out of leather.

↓ facts

Did you know that a person's
apostrophe for possession ↗

hands can also be used to create

puppets? In fact, anything

that will block part of the light

travelling from the light source

to the screen can be used!

The creation of a shadow ↓

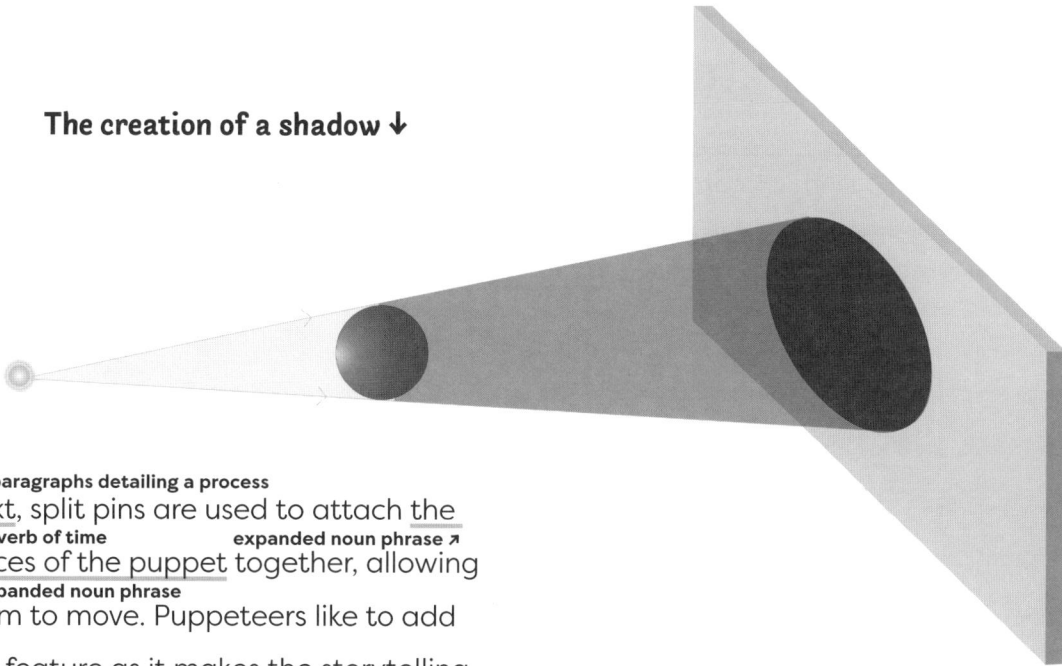

↓↑ **paragraphs detailing a process**

Next, split pins are used to attach the
↑ **adverb of time**   **expanded noun phrase** ↗
pieces of the puppet together, allowing
↖ **expanded noun phrase**
them to move. Puppeteers like to add

this feature as it makes the storytelling
                ↑ **subordinating conjunction**
more interesting.

↓↑ **paragraphs detailing a process**

Following that, the light source needs
↑ **adverbial of time**   **present tense** ↗
to be created, since the show will not
↖ **present tense**
work without it! Any light source can

be used, for example, a candle, a torch
                        comma for list ↑
or a lantern. Light travels in a straight

line and it will continue until it meets

an opaque (solid) object. The puppet is
        ↑ **technical vocabulary**
placed between the lamp and the screen
            subordinating conjunction ↓
to create a shadow. When the light's rays
                        apostrophe for possession ↑

↓↑ **paragraphs detailing a process**

are blocked, a shadow is made. Shadow

puppeteers' knowledge of this science is

used to successfully create their shows.
            ↑ **adverb of manner**
Interestingly, the closer the puppet is
↑ **word ending in -ly**
to the light, the more light waves are

blocked, so the bigger the shadow will be.

↓↑ **paragraphs detailing a process**

Finally, once the screen, puppets and
↑ **word ending in -ly**   ↑ **comma for list**
light source are all ready, the show can
        ↓→ **formal language**
begin. Moving the puppets behind
↓→ **formal language**
the screen creates the illusion that the
↓→ **formal language**
puppets are moving on their own. Very

talented and experienced puppeteers

can make the figures appear to walk,

talk, fight and even dance.

↓↑ **paragraphs detailing a process**

When the light source is removed, by

turning off the light, the shadows will

disappear and the show is over!

Year 4 overview

Use this overview and the checklist alongside the Year 4 model text (pages 50 – 53).

🐾 Specific features for this text type

• A clear title	*How did the Titanic sink?*
• An introductory paragraph – say what is going to be explained	*The truth behind the Titanic's final hours has intrigued people for many generations...*
• Paragraphs detailing a process, often in chronological order	
• Facts	*There are only twenty lifeboats on board.*
• Present tense	*At approximately 11:40 pm, the Titanic strikes an iceberg.*
• Formal language and technical vocabulary	*lifeboat, SOS signals, captain*

The following lists should be used as a tool to help teachers plan where to cover explicit grammar, punctuation and spelling objectives from both the Teacher Assessment Framework and the National Curriculum Programmes of Study.

🐾 Grammar

• Coordinating conjunctions – link ideas with 'and', 'but', 'so' and 'for'	*Most of the water is stopped, but some of it continues to enter.* *The ship raises the alarm for it needs to let the passengers know that they are in danger.*
• Subordinating conjunctions – expand upon independent clauses with 'when', 'as', 'before', 'since' and 'although' / 'even though'	*When it strikes the iceberg, the captain is alerted...* *Even though the water-tight doors have been closed, the water can still...*
• Expanded noun phrases – add detail to nouns	*the hull of the ship* *the water from the lower decks*
• Adverbs / adverbials of time	*approximately ___ minutes later*
• Adverbs / adverbials of manner – say how something is done	*In sheer panic, the people scramble to the lifeboats.* *In desperation, the passengers rush upon the lifeboat.*

🐾 Punctuation

- Commas for fronted adverbials   *During this time, the signals are not heard.*
- Commas for lists   *...destined for Cherbourg, Queenstown and New York.*
- Apostrophes for possession   *the captain's response, the ship's communications*

🐾 Spelling

- Year 3 / 4 words from the National Curriculum word lists: see page 9 of this book for a list of these. These words are highlighted in the Year 4 model text.
- Words ending in -ly   *rapidly, desperately, fearfully, continuously*
- Words ending in -tion   *consideration, desperation, hesitation*

🐾 Checklist

Use this checklist with the Year 4 model text. See page 7 for more information.

Title	
Introductory paragraph	
Paragraphs detailing a process	
Facts	
Present tense	
Formal language	
Technical vocabulary	
Grammar: Coordinating conjunctions	
Grammar: Subordinating conjunctions	
Grammar: Expanded noun phrases	
Grammar: Adverbs / adverbials of time	
Grammar: Adverbs / adverbials of manner	
Punctuation: Commas for fronted adverbials	
Punctuation: Commas for lists	
Punctuation: Apostrophes for possession	
Spelling: Year 3 / 4 word list	
Spelling: Words ending in -ly	
Spelling: Words ending in -tion	

Year 4 model text

How does the water cycle work?

Did you know that the water we drink today has been around for as long as the Earth? In fact, water never stops moving and is continuously being recycled.

Everybody knows that water is essential since all living things, including plants and animals, need it to survive. But where does it come from and where does it go?

There are four main stages of the recycling process which we refer to as the water cycle.

condensation

evaporation

Evaporation

As the water cycle is continuous, there is no real starting point! However, we will start with the process of evaporation. When warmth from the sun's rays heats up the water from the Earth's oceans, lakes, streams, ice and soils, it causes the water to rise into the air and turn into water vapour.

Condensation

Following that, the water vapour quickly cools as it rises in a process called condensation. As the water vapour cools down, it changes back into tiny drops of liquid water, merges with other water droplets and creates the clouds in our skies. There are various types of clouds including cirrus, stratus and cumulus.

precipitation

collection

> **?** *Did you know that the water cycle is essential to supporting all life on Earth? If we didn't have it, nothing would grow or survive!*

Precipitation

Before precipitation can take place in the form of rain or snow (or even hail or sleet), the clouds must become heavy. When the clouds reach the required weight, liquid water falls from them onto the Earth's surface. Precipitation is vital to our survival, although it can also be very damaging when too much rain falls and causes flooding.

Collection or run-off

Finally, the water from the rain or other forms of precipitation runs over the land, running downhill in streams, rivers and lakes. It collects in these places before flowing back to the seas and oceans, where the cycle starts all over again.

This is the water cycle. It is important to remember that without it, nothing would grow.

> **?** *Did you know that some parts of the cycle take hundreds of years to complete for some water is frozen in polar regions or located in some of the Earth's underground reservoirs?*

Year 4 model text: annotated

Dark grey highlights = Words from the National Curriculum word lists

How does the water cycle work?
↑ title

↓ introduction

Did you know that the water we drink today has been around for as long as the Earth? In fact, water never stops moving and is continuously being recycled.
↑ word ending in -ly

↓ present tense

Everybody knows that water is essential since all living things, including plants
↑ subordinating conjunction

and animals, need it to survive. But
coordinating conjunction ↑

where does it come from and where does it go?

There are four main stages of the recycling process which we refer to as the water cycle.

↓ word ending in -tion

Evaporation
↓ paragraphs detailing a process

As the water cycle is continuous, there is
↑ subordinating conjunction

no real starting point! However, we will start with the process of evaporation.
↑ expanded noun phrase

When warmth from the sun's rays heats
↑ subordinating conjunction

up the water from the Earth's oceans,
↑ apostrophe for possession

lakes, streams, ice and soils, it causes the
↑ commas for list

water to rise into the air and turn into

water vapour.

↓ word ending in -tion

Condensation
↓ paragraphs detailing a process   adverb of manner ↓

Following that, the water vapour quickly
↑ adverbial of time   ↖ comma for fronted adverbial

cools as it rises in a process called
↑ present tense

condensation. As the water vapour cools

condensation

evaporation

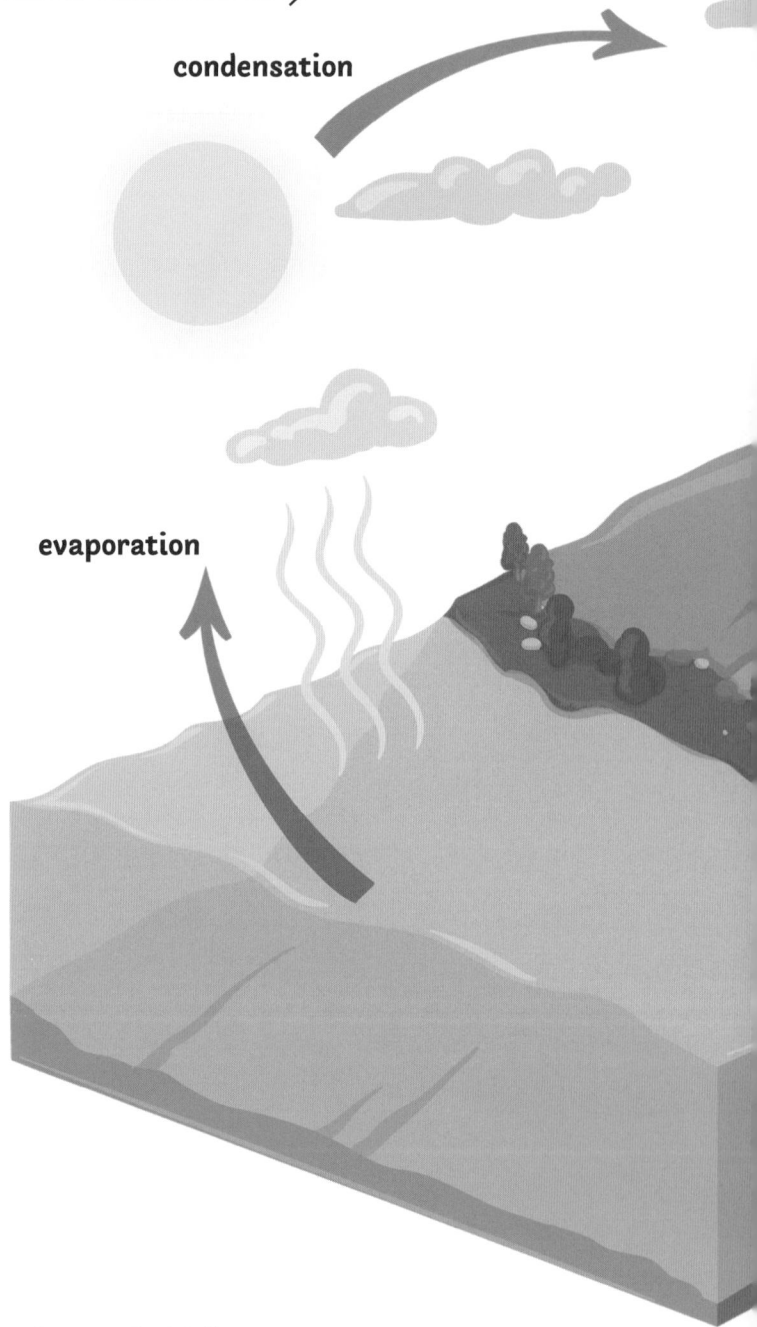

↓ paragraphs detailing a process

down, it changes back into tiny drops of liquid water, merges with other water droplets and creates the clouds in our skies. There are various types of clouds including cirrus, stratus and cumulus.
↑ technical vocabulary

precipitation

? *Did you know that the water cycle is essential to supporting all life on* Earth*? If we didn't have it, nothing would grow or survive!*

↓ word ending in -tion
Precipitation

↓ paragraphs detailing a process
Before precipitation can take place
↑ subordinating conjunction

in the form of rain or snow (or even

hail or sleet), the clouds must become

heavy. When the clouds reach the

required weight, liquid water falls
↑ comma for fronted adverbial

from them onto the Earth's surface.

Precipitation is vital to our survival,
↑ formal language

although it can also be very damaging
↑ subordinating conjunction

when too much rain falls and causes

flooding.

↓ word ending in -tion
Collection or run-off

↓ paragraphs detailing a process
Finally, the water from the rain or other
↑ word ending in -ly

forms of precipitation runs over the land,
↑ technical vocabulary

running downhill in streams, rivers and

lakes. It collects in these places before

flowing back to the seas and oceans,

where the cycle starts all over again.

collection

↓ facts
? *Did you know that some parts of the cycle take hundreds of years to* complete *for some water is*
↑ coordinating conjunction
frozen in polar regions or located in some of the Earth's
expanded noun phrase ↗
underground reservoirs?
↖ expanded noun phrase

↓ paragraphs detailing a process
This is the water cycle. It is important
formal language ↗

to remember that without it, nothing
↖ formal language

would grow.

Year 5 overview

Use this overview and the checklist alongside the Year 5 model text (pages 56 – 59).

🦖 Specific features for this text type

● A clear title	*What causes an earthquake?*
● An introductory paragraph – say what is going to be explained	*Earthquakes have caused havoc since the dawn of time...*
● Paragraphs detailing a process, often in chronological order	
● Facts	*Earthquakes occur when two large pieces of the Earth's crust rub together.*
● Present tense	*Shockwaves cause the surface of the Earth to shake.*
● Formal language	
● Technical vocabulary	*seismic, tectonic plates, crust*

The following lists should be used as a tool to help teachers plan where to cover explicit grammar, punctuation and spelling objectives from both the Teacher Assessment Framework and the National Curriculum Programmes of Study.

🦖 Grammar

● Subordinating conjunctions – expand upon independent clauses with 'when', 'as', 'before', 'since', 'until' and 'although' / 'even though'	*When two plates slide past each other, friction is created causing...* *Before it can be declared safe, authorities must ensure that...*
● Expanded noun phrases – add detail to nouns	*the mantle of the Earth's crust* *the largest fault surfaces on Earth*
● Relative clauses – embed extra information	*The Earth's surface, which is made up of numerous tectonic plates, is known...*
● Conjunctive adverbs for cause and effect – link connected points	*Consequently, the friction caused by the movement...*
● Adverbs / adverbials of time	*Immediately after, up to a day later, moments later*

🐾 Punctuation

- Punctuation for parentheses   *The location directly above where the earthquake starts, which is called the epicentre, is the...*

🐾 Spelling

- Year 5 / 6 words from the National Curriculum word lists: see page 9 of this book for a list of these. These words are highlighted in the Year 5 model text.
- Words ending in -ible   *reversible, responsible, feasible, plausible*
- Hyphenated words   *well-known, concrete-reinforced, high-tech*

🐾 Checklist

Use this checklist with the Year 5 model text. See page 7 for more information.

Title	
Introductory paragraph	
Paragraphs detailing a process	
Facts	
Present tense	
Formal language	
Technical vocabulary	
Grammar: Subordinating conjunctions	
Grammar: Expanded noun phrases	
Grammar: Relative clauses	
Grammar: Conjunctive adverbs for cause and effect	
Grammar: Adverbs / adverbials of time	
Punctuation: Punctuation for parentheses	
Spelling: Year 5 / 6 word list	
Spelling: Words ending in -ible	
Spelling: Hyphenated words	

Year 5 model text

How do volcanoes erupt?

Volcanoes are incredible things! In fact, they are responsible for creating more than eighty per cent of the Earth's physical landscape: mountains, craters and bleak terrains.

Despite being extremely dangerous, they are necessary for human life since the volcanic rocks they produce are home to precious nutrients. Remarkably, there are volcanoes on every continent – even Antarctica! Some of the most well-known examples include Mount Vesuvius, Krakatoa and Mount Etna. According to specialists, there are currently 1,500 potentially active volcanoes around the world, but how do they erupt?

Before a volcano can erupt, it first needs to be formed. Most of the volcanoes in the world have formed along the boundaries of the Earth's tectonic plates, which are pieced together like a huge jigsaw puzzle. When the tectonic plates collide into one another, one is often pushed below the other one.

As the landmass sinks into the Earth, temperatures and pressures increase which releases water from the rock – the mantle. This water decreases the melting point of the rocks above; consequently, magma is formed. This magma is lighter in weight than the rocks around it, so it continues to rise until it eventually reaches the surface. As the magma rises, bubbles of gas form inside it.

Next, the – now runny – magma erupts through openings or vents, which are located in the Earth's crust. Even though this liquid is referred to as magma when

The formation of a volcano →

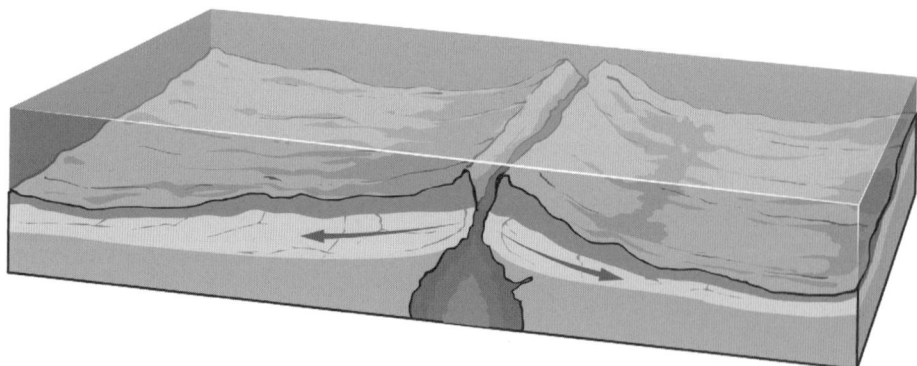

? *Do you know what the warning signs are for a volcano about to erupt? You might be able to recognise some of these warning signs as they might include small earthquakes, swelling or bulging of the volcano's sides and increased emission of gases from its vents. These warning signs don't necessarily mean that an eruption is guaranteed; however, they can help scientists prepare and evaluate the likelihood that an explosion might happen.*

it is liquid rock within the volcano, it becomes lava as it flows onto the Earth's surface.

If the magma is thick, the gas bubbles from within the dangerous liquid are unable to escape as easily and, as a result, the pressure increases as the molten rock continues to rise. Following that, once the pressure reaches a sufficient level, an explosive eruption can occur.

However, eruptions can also occur when tectonic plates are being pulled apart or when the water underneath the Earth's surface mixes with the hot magma. The interaction taking place in these deep-sea volcanoes causes steam to be produced. If this steam builds up enough pressure, an explosion is a definite end result!

As well as the magma forcing itself up in the form of lava, fragments of this boiling rock can also be driven upwards, filling the air. Frequently, additional, devastating events are then triggered including mudslides, avalanches, earthquakes and even tsunamis.

A cross-section of a volcano →

Year 5 model text: annotated

Dark grey highlights = Words from the National Curriculum word lists

How do volcanoes erupt?
↑ title

introduction / ↓ present tense

Volcanoes are incredible things! In fact, they are responsible for creating
↑ word ending in -ible   ↑ word ending in -ible
more than eighty per cent of the Earth's physical landscape: mountains,

craters and bleak terrains.

Despite being extremely dangerous, they are necessary for human life since the
subordinating conjunction ↑
volcanic rocks they produce are home to precious nutrients. Remarkably, there are volcanoes on every continent – even Antarctica! Some of the most well-
hyphenated word ↗
known examples include Mount Vesuvius,
↖ hyphenated word
Krakatoa and Mount Etna. According to specialists, there are currently 1,500 potentially active volcanoes around the
↑ technical vocabulary
world, but how do they erupt?

↓ paragraphs detailing a process
Before a volcano can erupt, it first needs
↑ adverbial of time
to be formed. Most of the volcanoes in the world have formed along the boundaries of the Earth's tectonic plates,
↑ technical vocabulary   comma for parenthesis ↑
which are pieced together like a huge
relative clause ↗
jigsaw puzzle. When the tectonic plates
↖ relative clause   ↑ subordinating conjunction

↓ paragraphs detailing a process
collide into one another, one is often pushed below the other one.

↓ paragraphs detailing a process
As the landmass sinks into the Earth,
↑ present tense
temperatures and pressures increase which releases water from the rock – the
dash for parenthesis ↗
mantle. This water decreases the melting
↖ dash for parenthesis
point of the rocks above; consequently,
conjunctive adverb for cause and effect ↑
magma is formed. This magma is lighter in weight than the rocks around it, so it continues to rise until it eventually
↑ subordinating conjunction
reaches the surface. As the magma rises,
subordinating conjunction ↑
bubbles of gas form inside it.
↑ expanded noun phrase

↓ paragraphs detailing a process
Next, the – now runny – magma erupts
↑ adverb of time
through openings or vents, which are
↑ relative clause
located in the Earth's crust. Even though this liquid is referred to as magma when

The formation of a volcano →

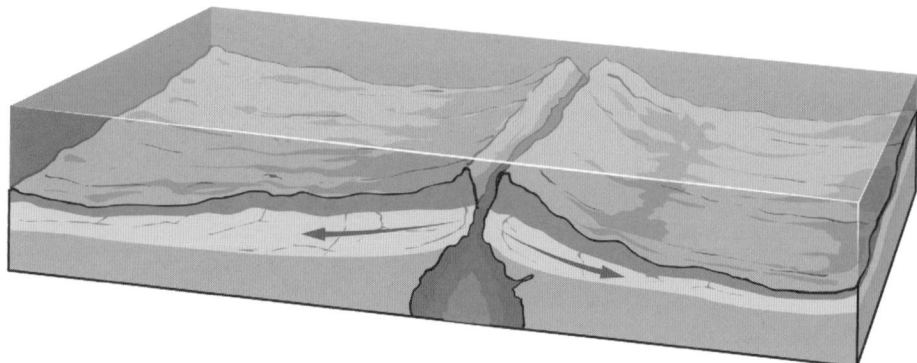

? **↑ facts**
Do you know what the warning signs are for a volcano about to erupt? You might be able to *recognise* some of these warning signs as they might include small earthquakes, swelling or bulging of the volcano's sides and increased emission of gases from its vents. These warning signs don't *necessarily* mean that an eruption is *guaranteed*; however, they can help scientists prepare and evaluate the likelihood that an explosion might happen.

it is liquid rock within the volcano, it becomes lava as it flows onto the Earth's surface.

If the magma is thick, the gas bubbles from within the dangerous liquid are unable to escape as easily and, as a result,
conjunctive adverb for cause and effect ↑
the pressure increases as the molten rock
technical vocabulary ↗
continues to rise. Following that, once
adverbial of time ↑
the pressure reaches a sufficient level, an
expanded noun phrase ↗
explosive eruption can occur.
↖ expanded noun phrase

↓ formal language
However, eruptions can also occur when tectonic plates are being pulled apart or

↓ ↑ formal language
when the water underneath the Earth's surface mixes with the hot magma. The interaction taking place in these deep-sea
hyphenated word ↑
volcanoes causes steam to be produced. If this steam builds up enough pressure, an explosion is a definite end result!

As well as the magma forcing itself up in the form of lava, fragments of this
expanded noun phrase ↗
boiling rock can also be driven upwards,
↖ expanded noun phrase **↑ present tense**
filling the air. Frequently, additional, devastating events are then triggered including mudslides, avalanches, earthquakes and even tsunamis.

A cross-section of a volcano →

Year 6 overview

Use this overview and the checklist alongside the Year 6 model texts (pages 62 – 69).

🐿 Specific features for this text type

• A clear title	*How does a hot air balloon take flight?*
• An introductory paragraph – say what is going to be explained	*Flight has transformed passenger travel ever since...*
• Paragraphs detailing a process, often in chronological order	
• Facts	*The temperature inside a hot air balloon is usually kept just below 120°C.*
• Present tense	*A hot air balloon consists of...*
• Formal language	
• Technical vocabulary	*burner, envelope, pilot, basket*

The following lists should be used as a tool to help teachers plan where to cover explicit grammar, punctuation and spelling objectives from both the Teacher Assessment Framework and the National Curriculum Programmes of Study.

🐿 Grammar

• Passive voice – to avoid a narrative-sounding structure	*The basket is attached to the balloon.*
• Subordinating conjunctions – expand upon independent clauses with 'when', 'as', 'before', 'since', 'until' and 'although' / 'even though'	*Since the balloon is large in size, two people are needed to hold it down.* *The balloon is filled until it is rounded and stretched.*
• Expanded noun phrases – add detail to nouns	*the mouth of the balloon* *the heat from the burner*
• Relative clauses – embed extra information	*The pilot, who is responsible for ensuring the safety of the passengers, operates the burner.*
• Conjunctive adverbs for cause and effect – link connected points	*Consequently, the balloon begins to descend.*
• Adverbs / adverbials of time	*After the balloon has started to inflate...*
• Evaluative adverbs	*incredibly, amazingly, weirdly*

🐾 Punctuation

- Semi-colons and colons *Pilot training requires experience: this mode of transport is dangerous.*

- Punctuation for parentheses *Baskets (usually made from wicker) carry...*

🐾 Spelling

- Year 5 / 6 words from the National Curriculum word lists: see page 9 of this book for a list of these. These words are highlighted in the Year 6 model texts.
- Words ending in -ible *possible, feasible, flexible, responsible*
- Words with hyphens *lesser-known, left-handed*

🐾 Checklist

Use this checklist with the Year 6 model texts. See page 7 for more information.

Title	
Introductory paragraph	
Paragraphs detailing a process	
Facts	
Present tense	
Formal language	
Technical vocabulary	
Grammar: Passive voice	
Grammar: Subordinating conjunctions	
Grammar: Expanded noun phrases	
Grammar: Relative clauses	
Grammar: Conjunctive adverbs for cause and effect	
Grammar: Adverbs / adverbials of time	
Grammar: Evaluative adverbs	
Punctuation: Semi-colons / colons	
Punctuation: Parentheses	
Spelling: Year 5 / 6 word list	
Spelling: Words ending in -ible	
Spelling: Words with hyphens	

Year 6 model text 1

How does blood circulate around the body?

The circulatory system is an essential part of the human body, but what is it?

If you hold your hand to your chest, you will be able to feel your heart beating. In fact, your heart beats around 100,000 times a day. Your circulatory system and your heart, which is a muscle about the size of your fist, cooperate in order to deliver blood to your organs; without them, you would not be able to survive!

The heart

What is the heart?

The heart is an organ, which is protected by the ribs. The heart acts a bit like a pump pushing blood around the body. According to scientists, it is one of the hardest-working muscles in the body as it must continuously pump about five litres (eight pints) of blood at a time!

The following process, which is also referred to as the cardiac cycle, is the sequence of events that takes place during one heartbeat.

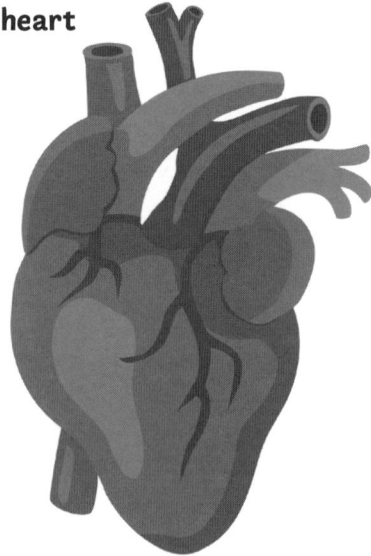

Before each beat of the heart, the organ, which is located slightly to the left of the chest, fills with blood. Since the heart is a muscle, it can contract – squeeze together – and force the blood away from the left-hand side of the heart in blood vessels, which are called arteries. Arteries are different from other blood vessels: they have thicker walls in order to withstand the pressure created by the blood as it leaves the heart. The oxygen-rich blood leaving the heart travels via the aorta (the main artery leaving the heart) and on to the rest of the body.

Once the blood has left the heart's left side, where the oxygenated blood is located, it travels to various parts of the human body. As it does so, the oxygen is removed by the body's cells and replaced with carbon dioxide, which is the waste product created when the cells use the oxygen. Incredibly, even though some of the cells are in hard-to-reach places, the blood can reach them by travelling through a network of much smaller blood vessels, known as capillaries.

Once the oxygenated blood has been carried around the body, it has completed its role; consequently, it needs to return to the heart. It does this by means of blood vessels, which are called veins.

Next, the returning, deoxygenated blood enters the right side of the heart through the vena cava. Once the blood is in the right ventricle, it is immediately pumped into the lungs, where the carbon dioxide is removed, and vacated from the body when we exhale. As we inhale, oxygen enters the lungs and is transferred to the blood in a process called 'diffusion'. This oxygenated blood is then transported to the heart and the whole process can start again!

Even though there are a variety of stages within this process, all of this takes an average of fifty-five to sixty seconds to complete!

Blood circulation ↓

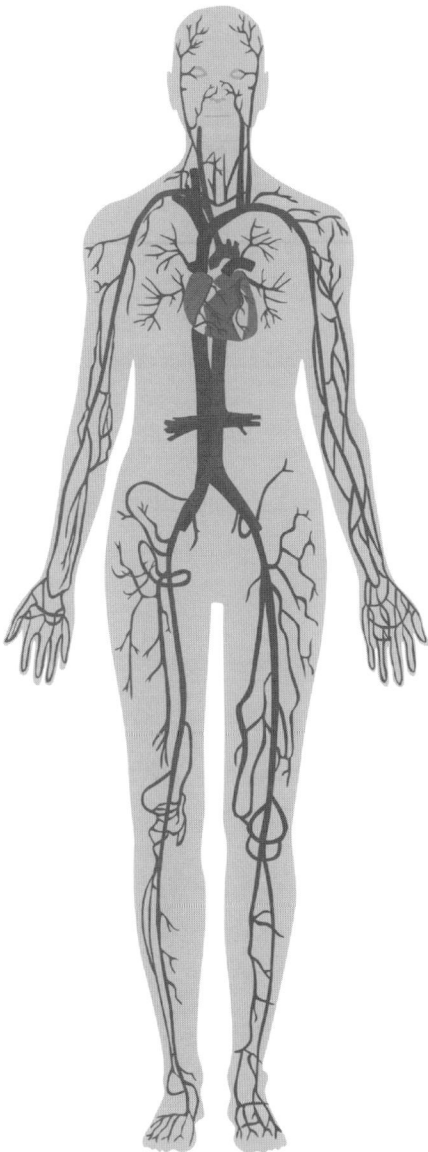

Chapter 2:
Explanation texts

Year 6 model text 1: annotated

Dark grey highlights = Words from the National Curriculum word lists

How does blood circulate around the body?
↑ title

↓ introduction
The circulatory system is an essential part of the human body, but what is it?

If you hold your hand to your chest, you will be able to feel your heart beating. In fact, your heart beats around 100,000 times a day. Your circulatory system and your heart, which is a
relative clause ↗
muscle about the size of your fist,
↖ relative clause
cooperate in order to deliver blood to your organs; without them, you would
semi-colon ↑
not be able to survive!

The heart

What is the heart?

The heart is an organ, which
↑ technical vocabulary
is protected by the ribs. The heart acts a bit like a pump pushing blood around the body. According to scientists, it
↓ facts
is one of the hardest-working muscles in the body as it must continuously pump about five litres (eight pints) of blood at a time!

↓ present tense
The following process, which is also referred to as the cardiac cycle, is the
expanded noun phrase ↗
sequence of events that takes place
↖ expanded noun phrase
during one heartbeat.

↓ paragraphs detailing a process
Before each beat of the heart, the
↑ adverbial of time
organ, which is located slightly to the left of the chest, fills with blood. Since
subordinating conjunction ↑
the heart is a muscle, it can contract
– squeeze together – and force the
↑ parenthesis   *↓ hyphenated word*
blood away from the left-hand side of
expanded noun phrase ↗
the heart in blood vessels, which are
↖ expanded noun phrase   *relative clause ↗*
called arteries. Arteries are different
↖ relative clause   *technical vocabulary ↗*
from other blood vessels: they have
↖ technical vocabulary   *↖ colon*
thicker walls in order to withstand the pressure created by the blood as it
subordinating conjunction ↑
leaves the heart. The oxygen-rich blood
↑ hyphenated word
leaving the heart travels via the aorta
(the main artery leaving the heart) and
↑ parenthesis
on to the rest of the body.

↓ **paragraphs detailing a process**
Once the blood has left the heart's
adverbial of time ↗
left side, where the oxygenated blood
↖ **adverbial of time**
is located, it travels to various parts

of the human body. As it does so, the
passive voice ↗
oxygen is removed by the body's cells
↖ **passive voice**
and replaced with carbon dioxide,

Blood circulation ↓

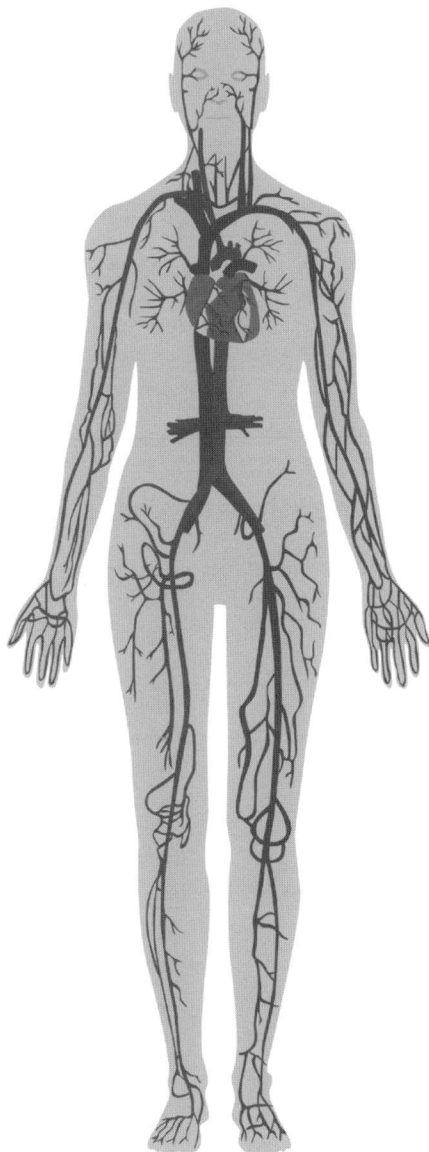

↓ **paragraphs detailing a process**
which is the waste product created

when the cells use the oxygen.
↑ **subordinating conjunction**
Incredibly, even though some of the cells
↑ **evaluative adverb**
are in hard-to-reach places, the blood
↑ **expanded noun phrase**
can reach them by travelling through

a network of much smaller blood

vessels, known as capillaries.
↑ **parenthesis**

↓ **paragraphs detailing a process**
Once the oxygenated blood has

been carried around the body, it has

completed its role; consequently, it
semi colon ↑   ↑ **conjunctive adverb for cause and effect**
needs to return to the heart. It does this

by means of blood vessels, which are

called veins.

↓ **paragraphs detailing a process**
Next, the returning, deoxygenated
↑ **adverb of time**
blood enters the right side of the heart
↑ **present tense**
through the vena cava. Once the blood
adverbial of time ↗
is in the right ventricle, it is immediately
↖ **adverbial of time**
pumped into the lungs, where the
relative clause ↗
carbon dioxide is removed, and vacated
↖ **relative clause**
from the body when we exhale. As we

inhale, oxygen enters the lungs and is

transferred to the blood in a process
↓→ **formal language** ─────→
called 'diffusion'. This oxygenated blood
↓→ **formal language** ─────→
is then transported to the heart and
↓→ **formal language** ─────→
the whole process can start again!

↓ **paragraphs detailing a process**
Even though there are a variety of
↑ **subordinating conjunction**   ↓→ **fact** ─→
stages within this process, all of this
↓→ **fact** ─→
takes an average of fifty-five
↑ **hyphenated word**
to sixty seconds to complete!
↑→ **fact** ─────→

Year 6 model text 2

How does the internet work?

In our modern world, the global computer network, which is generally referred to as the internet, is something that most of us take for granted in our everyday lives; it is easily accessible as it is available almost everywhere – well, apart from the South Pole!

If you've got a question, want to watch a music video or need to make contact with someone on the other side of the world, you can and in lightning speed! Mobile phones, computers, laptops and tablets are just some of the ways that the internet can be accessed to complete a whole variety of incredible things. But have you ever wondered how this well-known invention works? For instance, how can my computer in England 'speak' to your computer in Australia or send it my latest holiday photo?

The internet consists of millions of computers, which are digitally connected to each other by copper cables, fibres or wireless links. These computers are connected by means of a network, and it is via this network that your holiday photo can be sent.

Firstly, the image needs to be sent in a 'packet': a virtual parcel. When a large piece of information – such as a photo – is broken down into smaller pieces of information, it is called a 'packet'. These packets contain information about the image's data so that the picture can be reassembled. Each one of these packets includes a range of important information attached to it: where the data is going, where it has originated from and instructions regarding how to reassemble it.

Once the address is acquired, the packets are guided through the internet by special computers called routers; these are smart devices which direct or route information around the internet. The router can read the information on the data packet, before then sending it along the best possible route to its final destination. Even though these packets might have originated from the same computer, they can take different routes from each other and possibly will not arrive in the same order! However, distance is not a problem: packets can be sent across the world through fibre optic cables, which are located under the sea, or transmitted using satellites.

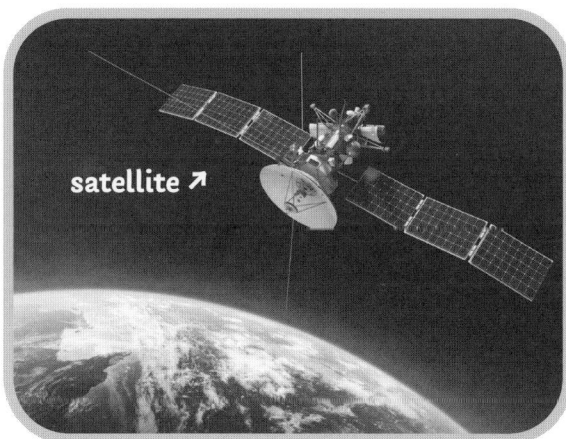

satellite ↗

As soon as the packets have been received, the web server opens them and reads the computer's request to open the image. Following that, the information, which is attached to the packets, explains to the computer how to reconstruct them. Consequently, an image will appear on the screen.

Since it usually takes less than a second to send and receive an image, it is easy to forget about the technology required to make it happen. The next time someone sends you a photo, think about how it got to your phone. A web server will have opened the packets of information and reconstructed the image. Larger files, such as videos, can take slightly longer to appear.

So, the next time you decide to send your latest holiday snap to a friend, I suggest that you think carefully about the amount of technology that is required to complete such a seemingly simplistic task!

? *Did you know that there are over 4.5 billion internet users in the world? That's 60% of the world's population.*

Year 6 model text 2: annotated

Dark grey highlights = Words from the National Curriculum word lists

How does the internet work?
↑ title

↓ introduction

In our modern world, the global computer network, which is generally referred
relative clause ↗
to as the internet, is
↖ relative clause   ↑ present tense
something that most of
↖ present tense
us take for granted in our
↖ present tense   ↓ semi-colon
everyday lives; it is easily
↓ subordinating conjunction
accessible as it is available
↑ word ending in -ible
almost everywhere – well,
parenthesis ↗
apart from the South Pole!
↖ parenthesis

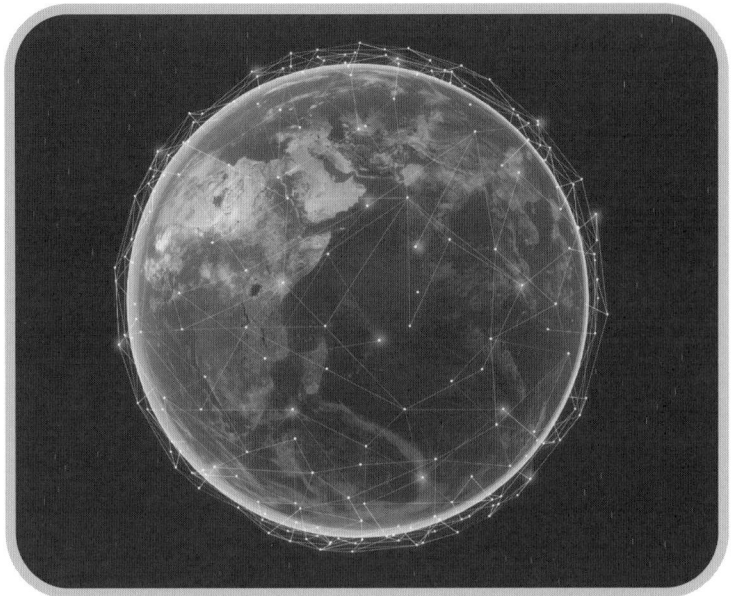

If you've got a question, want to watch a music video or need to make contact with someone on the other side of the
expanded noun phrase ↗
world, you can and in lightning speed!
↖ expanded noun phrase
Mobile phones, computers, laptops and tablets are just some of the ways that the internet can be accessed to complete a whole variety of incredible
word ending in -ible ↗
things. But have you ever wondered how this well-known invention works?
↑ hyphenated word
For instance, how can my computer in England 'speak' to your computer in Australia or send it my latest holiday photo?

↓ present tense
The internet consists of millions of computers, which are digitally connected
parenthesis ↗
to each other by copper cables, fibres
parenthesis ↗

↓↑ present tense
or wireless links. These computers are
↖ parenthesis   formal language ↗
connected by means of a network, and
↖ formal language
it is via this network that your holiday
passive voice ↗
photo can be sent.
↖ passive voice

↓ paragraphs detailing a process
Firstly, the image needs to be sent in
↑ adverb of time
a 'packet': a virtual parcel. When a large
colon ↑   subordinating conjunction ↑
piece of information – such as a photo
parenthesis ↗
– is broken down into smaller pieces of
↖ parenthesis   expanded noun phrase ↗
information, it is called a 'packet'. These
↖ expanded noun phrase   ↑ technical vocabulary
packets contain information about the image's data so that the picture can be reassembled. Each one of these packets includes a range of important information attached to it: where the
colon ↑
data is going, where it has originated from and instructions regarding how to reassemble it.

Grammarsaurus KS2© Mitch Hudson and Anna Richards 2021

Once the address is acquired, the
↑ **adverbial of time**
packets are guided through the internet
↑ **passive voice**
by special computers called routers;
semi-colon ↗
these are smart devices which direct or
route information around the internet.
The router can read the information on
the data packet, before then sending
it along the best possible route to its
↑ **word ending in -ible**
final destination. Even though these
↑ **subordinating conjunction**
packets might have originated from
the same computer, they can take
different routes from each other and
possibly will not arrive in the same order!
However, distance is not a problem:
↑ **conjunctive adverb**
packets can be sent across the world
through fibre optic cables, which are
formal language ↗
located under the sea, or transmitted
↖ **formal language**
using satellites.
↖ **formal language**

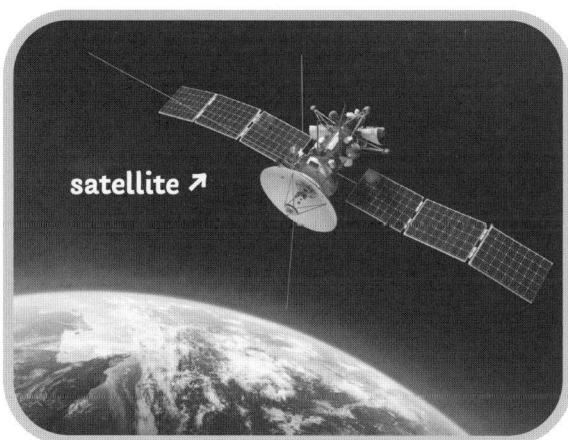

satellite ↗

As soon as the packets have been
adverbial of time ↗
received, the web server opens them
↖ **adverbial of time**
and reads the computer's request to
open the image. Following that, the
↑ **adverbial of time**
information, which is attached to the
parenthesis ↗
packets, explains to the computer how
↖ **parenthesis**
to reconstruct them. Consequently, an
↑ **conjunctive adverb for cause and effect**
image will appear on the screen.

Since it usually takes less than a second
to send and receive an image, it is
easy to forget about the technology
required to make it happen. The next
time someone sends you a photo, think
about how it got to your phone. A web
server will have opened the packets
of information and reconstructed the
image. Larger files, such as videos, can
↑ **parenthesis**
take slightly longer to appear.

So, the next time you decide to send
your latest holiday snap to a friend,
↑ **expanded noun phrase**
I suggest that you think carefully
about the amount of technology
that is required to complete
such a seemingly simplistic
task!

↓ **facts**
? *Did you know that there are over 4.5 billion internet users in the world? That's 60% of the world's population.*

Non-chronological reports

The purpose of a non-chronological report is to document and store information about a topic.

Tips for teaching children to write non-chronological reports

Children can find it easier to write a report based on their real-life experiences. When possible, consider how you could enable children to see or experience what they are going to write about. For example, could they visit a zoo before writing about wild animals?

If you are using a real-life stimulus, children will need to know key factual information to include in their report. Ask children to research a specific area and then 'interview' each other about the different topics to find out information in a more interesting way. For example, you might ask children to take notes whilst on a school trip or retrieve relevant information from simple books or information leaflets.

It can sometimes be difficult for children to focus on their writing skills if they are thinking too much about the content. Consider using a made-up context instead, so that children can focus on the grammar, punctuation and spelling rather than the factual details of a real-life event. For example, could they write a report about their own mythical creature or a new character for a book they have read?

Building cohesion from one paragraph to the next is a fundamental skill in writing a non-chronological report. Model how to do this by providing children with strips of paper, with the following on each strip:

- **Transition or introductory sentence**
- **Development sentences**
- **Ending sentence**

You could use the acronym TIDE for this: T stands for 'transition', I for 'introduction', D for 'development' and E for 'ending'.

To ensure that children are grouping relevant information in paragraphs, give children a paragraph to read and ask them to guess what the subheading might be. For example, can they read a paragraph about food an animal likes to eat and guess that the subheading is 'diet'? After they have written a paragraph, ask them to look at it again and think about whether a reader would be able to guess the subheading.

To scaffold writing about the appearance of a creature, use an image and label each part with the technical vocabulary so that this may be referred to during independent writing sessions, for example, labelling a bird of prey with 'sharp talons' and 'large wings'.

'Working at greater depth' explained

There are two texts for Year 6 level in this chapter. The second Year 6 text on pages 96 – 99 is designed to show 'greater depth'.

- A formal tone is adopted throughout.
- The passive voice is used ('much more is now known about this era'). Sentences with agentless passive constructions tend to be more formal and succinct.
- There are occasional sections with a direct address to the reader, for example, in the 'Did you know?' box.
- The text contains lots of facts and information, including dates.
- The text is organised into sub-sections, with each section flowing on from the next. For example, farmers are referred to at the end of the 'Power and Rule' paragraph and then there is a paragraph immediately afterwards focusing on farmers.
- Higher-level punctuation is used.
- Ambitious, technically-precise vocabulary has been selected.

Year 3 overview

Use this overview and the checklist alongside the Year 3 model text (pages 74 – 77).

🐾 Specific features for this text type

• A heading – introduce the topic	*Ancient Greece, Sparta and Athens, Minoan Crete*
• A brief introduction – general information	*Over 2,500 years ago...*
• Subheadings – organise the text into categories	
• Technical vocabulary	*architect, democracy, civilisation*
• Pictures and captions	
• Third person – formal	*Sparta and Athens united to fight against the Persian invasion.*
• Statements giving factual information	*The Minoans are considered to be the first civilisation of Europe.* *The Greeks held the first Olympic Games.*

The following lists should be used as a tool to help teachers plan where to cover explicit grammar, punctuation and spelling objectives from both the Teacher Assessment Framework and the National Curriculum Programmes of Study.

🐾 Grammar

• Coordinating conjunctions – link ideas with 'but', 'or', 'so', 'yet' or 'and'	*Many people believe that Ancient Greece was a united land, yet there were many city-states.*
• Subordinating conjunctions – expand upon independent clauses with 'even if', 'if', 'so that', 'when' or 'because'	*Athens and Sparta worked together so that they could defend themselves.*
• Expanded noun phrases – add detail to nouns with 'of', 'from', 'under', 'around', 'surrounding', 'next to', 'above' and 'with'	*the sea surrounding the Aegean Islands* *the warriors of Sparta*
• Present perfect tense	*Archaeologists have discovered that...*
• Collective nouns	*fleet, troop, army*

🐾 Punctuation

- Commas – for lists
  Greece was separated into city-states like Athens, Sparta, Corinth and Argos.

- Apostrophes for possession
  the city's defences, the ruler's plan, the general's attack

🐾 Spelling

- Year 3 / 4 words from the National Curriculum word lists: see page 9 of this book for a list of these. These words are highlighted in the Year 3 model text.

- Words ending in -ous
  enormous, tremendous, various

🐾 Checklist

Use this checklist with the Year 3 model text. See page 7 for more information.

Heading	
Brief introduction	
Subheadings	
Technical vocabulary	
Pictures and captions	
Third person – formal	
Statements giving factual information	
Grammar: Coordinating conjunctions	
Grammar: Subordinating conjunctions	
Grammar: Expanded noun phrases	
Grammar: Present perfect tense	
Grammar: Collective nouns	
Punctuation: Commas for lists	
Punctuation: Apostrophes for possession	
Spelling: Year 3 / 4 word list	
Spelling: Words ending in -ous	

Roman soldiers

The Roman army was a famous and important part of the Roman Empire. The soldiers in the Roman Empire came from Africa, Europe and the Middle East. Life was not easy for the men who joined the army. Can you imagine just how challenging a soldier's life could be?

How did soldiers train?

Life as a soldier was hard, and the soldiers' regular training needed to be very rigorous so that they were ready for action at any time. Historians have discovered that the hard-working fighters would attend training every morning to improve their skills when using a weapon. Some of the exercises included hand-to-hand combat with wooden swords, spears and shields. These were much heavier than the ones they used in conflict because it meant it would be easier when it came to the real battle.

Roman soldiers were expected to march long distances every day. During this march, soldiers were expected to carry a full pack of weapons, a shield, food rations, a cooking pot and a short spade, as well as their own personal

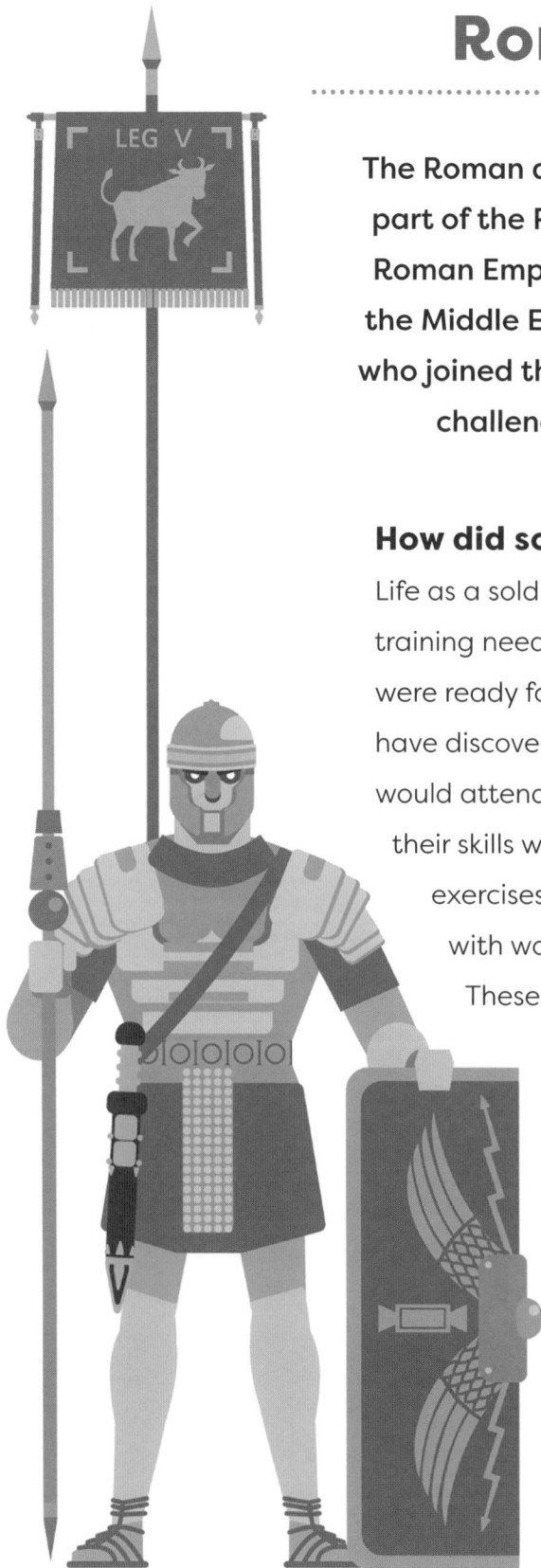

↓ **Roman legion**

possessions. Do you think you would be able to carry all of that? On top of this, they had to complete complex drills and learn different formations to support them in war.

How were they organised?

Historians have claimed that there were around half a million soldiers in the Roman army so they needed to be divided up to keep the men in order! These groups were called legions and each legion had about five thousand men. These groups were then divided further into centuries, led by a centurion. He was allowed to beat anyone who misbehaved with a short rod! A legion had commanders, officers and ordinary soldiers alongside other people such as doctors.

Roman soldiers were not always at war, yet even when they were just training, the leaders were incredibly strict. Soldiers had to be brave if they were going to break any rules or fall asleep on duty, because the punishment for any misbehaviour was very harsh.

Do you think you would be fit for life as a Roman soldier?

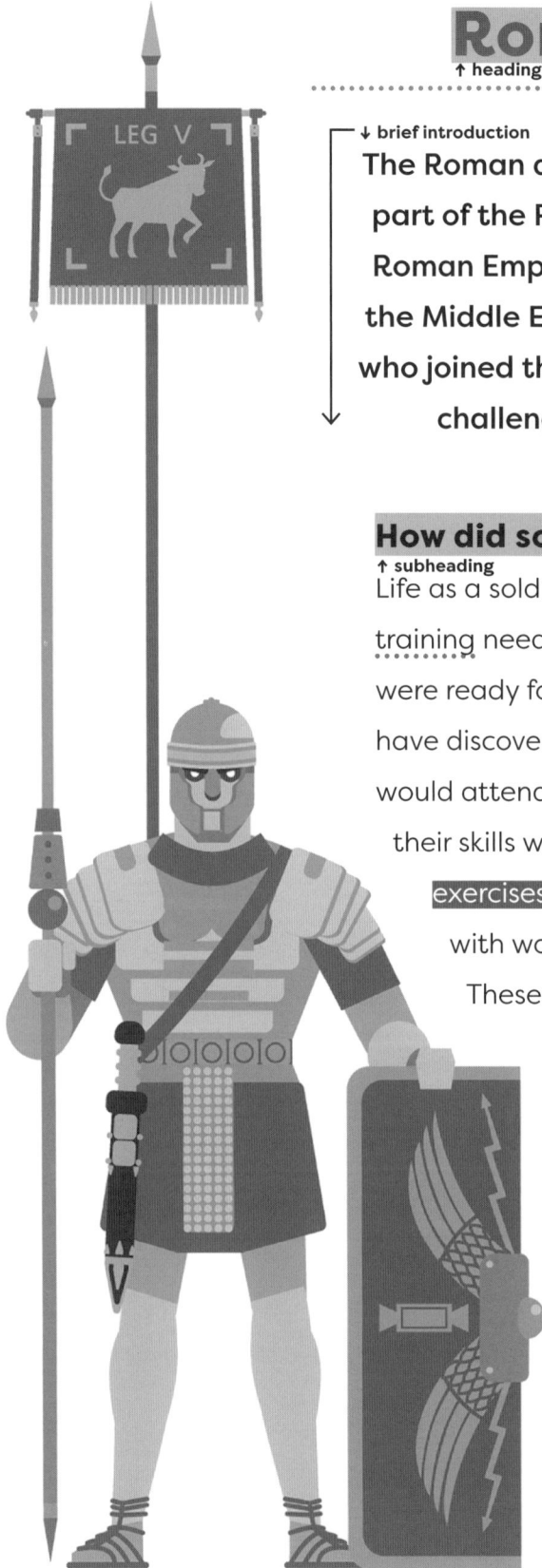

Year 3 model text: annotated

Dark grey highlights = Words from the National Curriculum word lists

Roman soldiers
↑ heading ──────────────→

↓ brief introduction

The Roman army was a famous and important
↑ word ending in -ous

part of the Roman Empire. The soldiers in the

Roman Empire came from Africa, Europe and
comma for list ↗

the Middle East. Life was not easy for the men

who joined the army. Can you imagine just how

challenging a soldier's life could be?

How did soldiers train?
↑ subheading

Life as a soldier was hard, and the soldiers' regular
↑ apostrophe for possession

training needed to be very rigorous so that they
word ending in -ous ↑ ↑ subordinating conjunction

were ready for action at any time. Historians

have discovered that the hard-working fighters
↑ expanded noun phrase

would attend training every morning to improve

their skills when using a weapon. Some of the

exercises included hand-to-hand combat
↑ technical vocabulary

with wooden swords, spears and shields.
↖ comma for list

These were much heavier than the ones

they used in conflict because it
↑ subordinating conjunction

meant it would be easier when

it came to the real battle.

Roman soldiers were expected to

march long distances every day.

During this march, soldiers were
formal language ↗

expected to carry a full pack of
↖ formal language

weapons, a shield, food rations,

a cooking pot and a short spade,

as well as their own personal

↓ Roman legion

possessions. Do you think you would be able to carry all of that? On top of this, they had to complete complex drills and learn different formations to
↑ coordinating conjunction
support them in war.

How were they organised?

Historians have claimed
↑ present perfect
that there were around half a million soldiers in the Roman army so they needed to be
↑ coordinating conjunction
divided up to keep the men in order! These groups were called legions and each
↑ technical vocabulary
legion had about five thousand men. These

groups were then divided further into centuries, led by a centurion.
↑ technical vocabulary
He was allowed to beat anyone who misbehaved with a short rod! A legion
collective noun ↑
had commanders, officers and ordinary
comma for list ↑
soldiers alongside other people such as doctors.

Roman soldiers were not always at
↓ coordinating conjunction   third person ↗
war, yet even when they were just
↖ third person
training, the leaders were incredibly strict. Soldiers had to be brave if they were going to break any rules or fall asleep on duty, because the punishment for any misbehaviour was very harsh.

Do you think you would be fit for life as a Roman soldier?
↑ expanded noun phrase

Year 4 overview

Use this overview and the checklist alongside the Year 4 model text (pages 80 – 83).

🐾 Specific features for this text type

• A heading – introduce the topic	*Famous sights across the globe*
• A brief introduction – general information	*The world-renowned Eiffel Tower was constructed in...* *How many famous landmarks have you visited?*
• Subheadings – organise the text into categories	
• Technical vocabulary	*structure, statue, marble, plinth, temple, column*
• Pictures and captions	
• Third person – formal	*The construction of the Acropolis began...*
• Statements giving factual information	*There are more than 20,000 watchtowers along the Great Wall of China.*

The following lists should be used as a tool to help teachers plan where to cover explicit grammar, punctuation and spelling objectives from both the Teacher Assessment Framework and the National Curriculum Programmes of Study.

🐾 Grammar

• Coordinating conjunctions – link ideas with 'but', 'or', 'so', 'yet' or 'and'	*The Leaning Tower of Pisa is a major tourist attraction and it was built over 800 years ago.*
• Subordinating conjunctions – expand upon independent clauses with 'even if', 'if', 'so that', 'when' or 'because'	*When the Temple of Kukulcan was first built, it was a wooden structure and not the...*
• Expanded noun phrases – add detail to nouns with 'of', 'from', 'under', 'around', 'surrounding', 'next to', 'above' and 'with'	*the bodies of the pharaohs* *the water surrounding the statue*
• Present perfect tense	*Scientists have discovered that...*

🐾 Punctuation

- Commas – for lists | *The statue represents liberty, friendship and freedom.*

- Apostrophes for possession | *the monument's exterior*
  the bridge's foundation

- Commas after fronted adverbials | *When it was first built,*
  After construction had been completed,

🐾 Spelling

- Year 3 / 4 words from the National Curriculum word lists: see page 9 of this book for a list of these. These words are highlighted in the Year 4 model text.

- Words ending in -ous | *hideous, various, glamorous, enormous, famous, mountainous*

🐾 Checklist

Use this checklist with the Year 4 model text. See page 7 for more information.

Heading	
Brief introduction	
Subheadings	
Technical vocabulary	
Pictures and captions	
Third person – formal	
Statements giving factual information	
Grammar: Coordinating conjunctions	
Grammar: Subordinating conjunctions	
Grammar: Expanded noun phrases	
Grammar: Present perfect tense	
Punctuation: Commas for lists	
Punctuation: Apostrophes for possession	
Punctuation: Commas after fronted adverbials	
Spelling: Year 3 / 4 word list	
Spelling: Words ending in -ous	

Year 4 model text

The Titanic

Built in Belfast, set sail from Southampton and destined for New York, this world-famous passenger ship sailed the Atlantic Ocean for just four days before it met a catastrophic end in April, 1912.

Back then, it was hailed as the 'unsinkable' Titanic, and this gigantic ocean liner measured an amazing 269 metres long, which made it the largest passenger ship on Earth at the time. But unfortunately, its size, power and strength on the ocean were no match for the tragedy that struck the 2,240 people aboard this 'ship of dreams'.

and built in Belfast. They wanted to build the biggest, grandest ship of all time and it took thousands of men over two years to build. Its enormous size and luxurious design cost an unbelievable amount of money – a reported £1,500,000 (£120,000,000 today).

Ambitious beginnings

A large shipping company, called the White Star Line, ordered for the ocean liner to be designed by Thomas Andrews

Four days aboard the Titanic

On April 10th 1912, the Titanic set sail from Southampton, England, where it then stopped at Cherbourg, France, followed by Queenstown, Ireland. After it had made its final stop in Ireland, the ship was expected to make the 137-hour journey to New York City. The vessel would only sail for three days across the Atlantic Ocean from Queenstown before it hit an iceberg late on April 14th.

↑ The Titanic's route

Abandon ship!

At around 11:40 pm, the ship's lookout, Frederick Fleet, spotted a large iceberg. Sadly, with only thirty-seven seconds before the ship would hit the object, the 'ship of dreams' managed only to turn slightly, causing a 300-foot-long line of damage along the hull of the boat. The ice-cold waters of the Atlantic Ocean flooded the first five compartments. The weight of the water made the front of the ship bow down into the sea, allowing even more water to rush into the vessel, causing it to sink even faster into the icy waters.

Just minutes after midnight, Captain Edward Smith ordered for the passengers to be brought up onto the deck to escape the sinking ship. Tragically, the design of the ship had allowed only 20 lifeboats to be on board – this was enough for 1,178 people. This left over 1,000 people with no chance of escaping the ship. To make matters worse, the crew of the ship were worried that the lifeboats would be too crowded if they put too many people into them. This meant that some lifeboats left the sinking ship with just 28 people on board.

The Titanic's final moments and lasting legacy

Whilst the passengers scrambled to get onto lifeboats, water continued to pull the front of the ship lower and lower into the darkness of the ocean.

After a few hours, the front of the ship was so heavy that the ship split in half and mere minutes later, the Titanic disappeared into the frozen depths of the Atlantic Ocean. This was just 2 hours and 40 minutes after it had hit the iceberg. 1,500 people did not survive the sinking.

Since the disaster, the Titanic has inspired countless paintings, poems and films.

Year 4 model text: annotated

Dark grey highlights = Words from the National Curriculum word lists

The Titanic
↑ heading →

↓ brief introduction

Built in Belfast, set sail from
↑ comma for list
Southampton and destined for New
York, this world-famous passenger
↑ word ending in -ous
ship sailed the Atlantic Ocean
for just four days before it met a
catastrophic end in April, 1912.

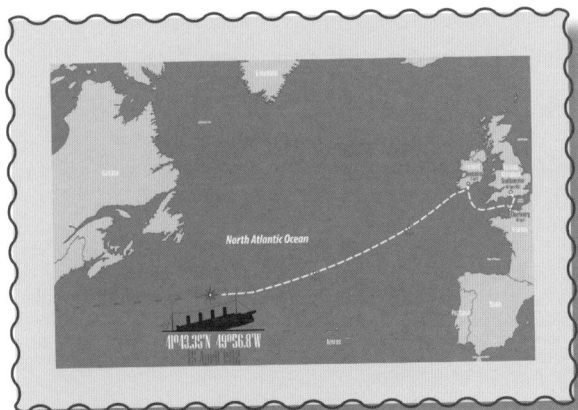

Back then, it was hailed as the
'unsinkable' Titanic, and this gigantic
ocean liner measured an amazing 269
↑ technical vocabulary
metres long, which made it the largest
expanded noun phrase ↗
passenger ship on Earth at the time.
↖ expanded noun phrase
But unfortunately, its size, power and
↑ comma for list
strength on the ocean were no match for
the tragedy that struck the 2,240 people
aboard this 'ship of dreams'.

Ambitious beginnings

A large shipping company, called the
↑ formal language
White Star Line, ordered for the ocean
liner to be designed by Thomas Andrews

↑ **The Titanic's route**

and built in Belfast. They wanted to build
↑ formal language
the biggest, grandest ship of all time and
↑ expanded noun phrase   coordinating conjunction ↑
it took thousands of men over two years
word ending in -ous ↓
to **build**. Its enormous size and luxurious
↑ word ending in -ous
design cost an unbelievable amount
of money – a reported £1,500,000
(£120,000,000 today).

Four days aboard the Titanic
↑ subheading

On April 10th 1912, the Titanic set
sail from Southampton, England,
where it then stopped at Cherbourg,
France, followed by Queenstown,
↓ subordinating conjunction
Ireland. After it had made its final stop
in Ireland, the ship was expected to
formal language ↗
make the 137-hour journey to New York
↖ formal language
City. The vessel would only sail for three
days across the Atlantic Ocean from
Queenstown before it hit an iceberg
↑ subordinating conjunction
late on April 14th.

Abandon ship!

At around 11:40 pm, the ship's lookout, *apostrophe for possession ↓*
comma for fronted adverbial ↗
Frederick Fleet, spotted a large iceberg.

Sadly, with only thirty-seven seconds before the ship would hit the object, the 'ship of dreams' managed only to turn slightly, causing a 300-foot-long line of damage along the hull of the boat. The
↑ technical vocabulary
ice-cold waters of the Atlantic Ocean flooded the first five compartments. The weight of the water made the front of the ship bow down into the sea, allowing even more water to rush into the vessel, causing it to sink even faster into the icy waters.

Just minutes after midnight, Captain *third person ↓*
comma for fronted adverbial ↗
Edward Smith ordered for the
↖ third person
passengers to be brought up onto the deck to escape the sinking ship. Tragically, the design of the ship had allowed only 20 lifeboats to be on
↑ technical vocabulary
board – this was enough for 1,178 people. This left over 1,000 people
↑→ factual information ─────
with no chance of escaping the ship.
↑→ factual information ─────
To make matters worse, the crew of the ship were worried that the lifeboats would be too crowded if they put too
subordinating conjunction ↗
many people into them. This meant that some lifeboats left the sinking ship with just 28 people on board.

The Titanic's final moments and lasting legacy

Whilst the passengers scrambled to
↑ subordinating conjunction
get onto lifeboats, water continued
↑→ third person ─────→
to pull the front of the ship lower and
↑→ third person ─────→
lower into the darkness of the ocean.
↑→ third person ─────→

After a few hours, the front of the *expanded noun phrase ↓*
comma for fronted adverbial ↗
ship was so heavy that the ship split
↖ expanded noun phrase
in half and mere minutes later, the Titanic disappeared into the frozen depths of the Atlantic Ocean. This was just 2 hours and 40 minutes after it had hit the iceberg. 1,500 people did
↑→ factual information →
not survive the sinking.
↑→ factual information ─────→

Since the disaster, the Titanic has inspired countless paintings,
↑ present perfect
poems and films.

Year 5 overview

Use this overview and the checklist alongside the Year 5 model text (pages 86 – 89).

🐾 Specific features for this text type

• A heading – introduce the topic	*Uncovering the hidden life of the swan-giraffe*
• A brief introduction – general information	*The elusive swan-giraffe has baffled zoologists for centuries...*
• Subheadings – organise the text into categories	
• Technical vocabulary	*diet, habitat, appearance, skeleton, talons*
• Pictures and captions	
• Third person – formal	*The wingspan of this vicious creature is believed to be...*
• Statements giving factual information	*Many swan-giraffes roam in small groups called rumbas.*

The following lists should be used as a tool to help teachers plan where to cover explicit grammar, punctuation and spelling objectives from both the Teacher Assessment Framework and the National Curriculum Programmes of Study.

🐾 Grammar

• Subordinating conjunctions – expand upon independent clauses with 'even if', 'if', 'so that', 'wherever', 'whenever' and 'when'	*Whenever a swan-giraffe encounters...*
• Relative clauses – embed extra information	*These beasts, which nest in the Amazon rainforest, often...*
• Conjunctive adverbs	
○ Additional points	*They use their feathers to impress their mates; in the same way, they use their beaks to...*
○ Similar points	*These creatures are often quite solitary; furthermore, due to their aggressive nature...*
○ Opposite points	*They mostly sleep in pairs; however, some prefer...*
○ Results	*They have more teeth than any other creature: as a result, their jaw weighs...*
○ Transition phrases	*With regards to diet...*
○ Summarising phrases	*In short, if you spot...*

🐾 Punctuation

• Commas for lists	*rabbits, rodents and cockroaches*
• Apostrophes for possession	*the creature's beak* *zoologists' findings*
• Parentheses with brackets, commas or dashes	*Its tail, which is covered in fur, is used to...*

🐾 Spelling

- Year 5 / 6 words from the National Curriculum word lists: see page 9 of this book for a list of these. These words are highlighted in the Year 5 model text.
- Words ending in -cious / -tious   *vicious, malicious, cautious, atrocious, ferocious, nutritious*

🐾 Checklist

Use this checklist with the Year 5 model text. See page 7 for more information.

Heading	
Brief introduction	
Subheadings	
Technical vocabulary	
Pictures and captions	
Third person – formal	
Statements giving factual information	
Grammar: Subordinating conjunctions	
Grammar: Relative clauses	
Grammar: Conjunctive adverbs	
Punctuation: Commas for lists	
Punctuation: Apostrophes for possession	
Punctuation: Parentheses	
Spelling: Year 5 / 6 word list	
Spelling: Words ending in -cious / -tious	

Year 5 model text

Ancient Greek myths: the cyclops

Even if they are not experts in Ancient Greek mythology, most people
are likely to recognise the name 'cyclops'. These vicious creatures,
who famously possessed neither social manners nor fear of the gods,
were generally thought of as monsters.

Appearance

Frequently described as wild savages, cyclopes (or cyclops in its singular form) were instantly identifiable due to their physical form. They were famous for their giant eye, which is located in the middle of their foreheads. The word 'cyclops' actually means 'round eye'. It is not clear where the idea about a one-eyed monster originated. Some believe it could be based on blacksmiths, who would cover one eye with an eye patch while they worked so that they were protected from sparks. Other legends assert that it could be related to the discovery of elephant skulls: the giant nasal cavities on the skulls might have been mistaken for eye sockets.

Elephant skull →

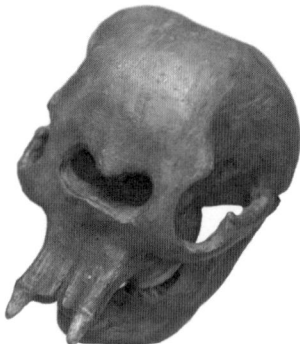

It is thought that the giant eye was the cyclops' only weak spot, as its skin, which is human-like in colour and texture, was much tougher than a person's. The size of a cyclops varied depending on the source. However, they were generally double the size of a human man (230 cm or 7.5 feet). As a result of their large size, these aggressive beasts were prone to laziness and inactivity, which was why they were often covered with insects and filth, due to a lack of bathing.

Habitat

In myths and legends, cyclopes were workers, whose workshops were in the heart of different volcanic mountains (including Etna). These monsters resided below the ground, where they would spend their time making huge tools and massive weapons. Using their weapons of thunder and lightning, the beasts would occupy the volcanic chambers and use their immense strength to forge

Diet

Are you wondering what these wild savages ate? They were known to be omnivores (an animal that eats both meat and vegetation) but, in reality, they preferred feasting on raw flesh, which came from animals they had recently slaughtered. Cyclopes generally ate what was available to them (sheep and cows), unless humans appeared – in which case they would devour them instead! In addition to this, they enjoyed drinking strong wine – when they could obtain it – which could send them to sleep.

In short, it is clear that cyclopes were monstrous brutes, to be avoided at all costs!

different legendary items including Hades' helmet of invisibility, Artemis' bow and arrows of moonlight and Poseidon's trident. Moreover, it is claimed that the pounding of their humongous hammers, which they used to create their weapons, caused earthquakes on the ground above them. Furthermore, the extreme temperatures from their furnaces would cause the volcanoes on the ground to erupt wherever their workshops were located.

Defeating a cyclops

Odysseus, one of the most famous heroes in Greek mythology, was captured by a cyclops on an island. He came up with a plan to defeat the cyclops by blinding him and escaping from the island.

Year 5 model text: annotated

Dark grey highlights = Words from the National Curriculum word lists

Ancient Greek myths: the cyclops

↑ heading

↓ brief introduction

Even if they are not experts in Ancient Greek mythology, most people

↑ subordinating conjunction

are likely to recognise the name 'cyclops'. These vicious creatures,

↑ word ending in -cious

who famously possessed neither social manners nor fear of the gods,

↑ relative clause

were generally thought of as monsters.

Appearance

↑ subheading

Frequently described as wild savages, cyclopes (or cyclops in its singular form) were instantly identifiable due to their physical form.

↓→ third person

They were famous for

↓→ third person

their giant eye, which is located in the

↓→ third person   relative clause ↗

middle of their foreheads. The word

↖ relative clause

'cyclops' actually means 'round eye'. It is not clear where the idea about a one-eyed monster originated. Some believe it could be based on blacksmiths, who would cover one eye with an eye patch while they worked so that they were

↑ subordinating conjunction

protected from sparks. Other legends

statements giving factual information ↗

assert that it could be related to the

↖ statements giving factual information

discovery of elephant skulls: the giant

↖ statements giving factual information

nasal cavities on the skulls might have

↖ statements giving factual information

been mistaken for eye sockets.

↖ statements giving factual information

Elephant skull →

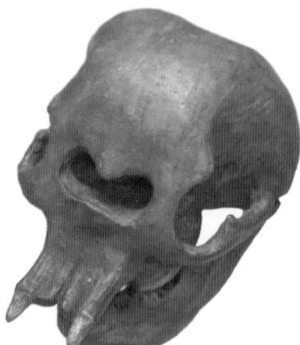

It is thought that the giant eye was the cyclops' only weak spot, as its skin, which is human-like in colour and

relative clause ↗

texture, was much tougher than a

↖ relative clause

person's. The size of a cyclops varied

↑ apostrophe for possession

depending on the source. However,

conjunctive adverb ↑

they were generally double the size of a human man (230 cm or 7.5 feet).

brackets for parenthesis ↑

As a result of their large size, these

↑ conjunctive adverb

aggressive beasts were prone to laziness and inactivity, which was why they were often covered with insects and filth, due to a lack of bathing.

Habitat

In myths and legends, cyclopes were workers, whose workshops were in the

relative clause ↗

heart of different volcanic mountains

↖ relative clause

(including Etna). These monsters resided below the ground, where they would

relative clause ↗

spend their time making huge tools and

↖ relative clause

massive weapons. Using their weapons

↖ relative clause

of thunder and lightning, the beasts would occupy the volcanic chambers and use their immense strength to forge

Diet

Are you wondering what these wild savages ate? They were known to
formal language ↗
be omnivores (an animal that eats
↖ formal language
both meat and vegetation) but, in reality, they preferred feasting on raw flesh, which came from animals they had recently slaughtered. Cyclopes generally ate what was available to them (sheep and cows), unless humans appeared – in which case they would
↑ formal language
devour them instead! In addition to this, they enjoyed drinking strong wine – when they could obtain it – which could
↑ dashes for parenthesis
send them to sleep.

↓ conjunctive adverb
In short, it is clear that cyclopes were
statements giving factual information ↗
monstrous brutes, to be avoided at
↖ statements giving factual information
all costs!

different legendary items including Hades' helmet of invisibility, Artemis' bow
comma for list ↗
and arrows of moonlight and Poseidon's trident. Moreover, it is claimed that
↑ conjunctive adverb
the pounding of their humongous hammers, which they used to create
↑ comma for parenthesis
their weapons, caused earthquakes on the ground above them. Furthermore,
conjunctive adverb ↗
the extreme temperatures from their furnaces would cause the volcanoes
↑ technical vocabulary
on the ground to erupt wherever their
subordinating conjunction ↑
workshops were located.

Defeating a cyclops

Odysseus, one of the most famous heroes in Greek mythology, was captured by a cyclops on an island. He came up with a plan to defeat the cyclops by blinding him and escaping from the island.

Year 6 overview

Use this overview and the checklist alongside the Year 6 model texts (pages 92 – 99).

🐾 Specific features for this text type

- A heading – introduce the topic — *Women and the Second World War*
- A brief introduction – general information — *Due to a large proportion of men being enlisted, women...*
- Subheadings – organise the text into categories
- Technical vocabulary — *authoritarian, Women's Land Army, conscientious objector*
- Third person – formal — *Using advanced weaponry, the army prepared...*
- Statements giving factual information — *One third of London was destroyed during the Blitz.*

The following lists should be used as a tool to help teachers plan where to cover explicit grammar, punctuation and spelling objectives from both the Teacher Assessment Framework and the National Curriculum Programmes of Study.

🐾 Grammar

- Passive voice — *The response was organised by...*
- Subordinating conjunctions – expand upon independent clauses with 'even if', 'if', 'so that', 'whenever' and 'when' — *If air raid signals sounded, citizens knew to immediately find shelter.*
- Relative clauses – embed extra information — *The Luftwaffe, which was the German equivalent of the RAF, was led by...*
- Subjunctive mood/form — *If a threat were to present itself...*
- Conjunctive adverbs
  - Additional points — *RAF squadrons were deployed to protect the South coast; in addition to this, the AA guns and spotters worked to...*
  - Similar points — *Radar operatives communicated directly with plotters to assemble the defence; similarly, the spotters across Britain fed back...*
  - Opposite points — *Some German generals argued for an immediate naval invasion; on the other hand, Hitler and Goering preferred an aerial assault...*
  - Results — *Major cities were under attack: consequently, children were evacuated...*
  - Transition phrases — *As far as aerial defence is concerned...*
  - Summarising phrases — *In summary, the war was...*

Grammarsaurus KS2© Mitch Hudson and Anna Richards 2021

🐾 Punctuation

• Semi-colons	*The majority of Britain supported...; a small minority opposed...*
• Colons	*The German war machine was unstoppable: Hitler had conquered most of Europe by 1941.*
• Apostrophes for possession	*the plane's engine, the commander's strategy*
• Parentheses with brackets, commas or dashes	*The Luftwaffe, which was the German equivalent of the RAF, was led by...*

🐾 Spelling

- Year 5 / 6 words from the National Curriculum word lists: see page 9 of this book for a list of these. These words are highlighted in the Year 6 model texts.

• Words ending in -cious, -tious and -ous	*infectious, conscious, victorious, rebellious*

🐾 Checklist

Use this checklist with the Year 6 model texts. See page 7 for more information.

Heading	
Brief introduction	
Subheadings	
Technical vocabulary	
Third person – formal	
Statements giving factual information	
Grammar: Passive voice	
Grammar: Subordinating conjunctions	
Grammar: Relative clauses	
Grammar: Subjunctive mood/form	
Grammar: Conjunctive adverbs	
Punctuation: Semi-colons / colons	
Punctuation: Apostrophes for possession	
Punctuation: Parentheses	
Spelling: Year 5 / 6 word list	
Spelling: Words ending in -cious, -tious and -ous	

Year 6 model text 1

The ancient Maya

The ancient Maya were a civilisation that thrived between 2000 BC and AD 1500.

Their city-states spread across Mesoamerica, which is Southern Mexico and Central America today. Considered to be extremely advanced for their time, the Maya are still known for their writing, art, science and architecture. Their temples and pyramids can still be found in the jungles of Central America. Strangely, many of the Maya cities were abandoned in the 10th century, which confuses many archaeologists to this day. What could have happened to these powerful city-states?

? *Did you know? The Maya built pyramids to get closer to the gods.*

How did the Maya civilisation start to grow?

Life was not straightforward during these times, as the Mesoamerican region was not the most forgiving; although it was fertile, the soil was not very deep and torrential rainfall washed it away in hilly areas during the rainy season.

In the lowlands, there were only two seasons – rainy or dry. Because of this, people had to store water to drink and could only grow crops during the rainy season. The Maya invented a genius way to collect and store water for drinking and, in places, to irrigate their farmland – aguadas. These were man-made lakes often lined with lime to prevent the water from seeping through the porous stone below. The Maya even designed their cities so that water would drain into the aguada.

With regards to hilly areas, the Maya constructed terraced farms. This clever technique was used to build farms on steep hills creating a flat surface to grow on, and it stopped the soil from sliding away.

With a plentiful supply of water, crops and an abundance of natural limestone – a natural material used for building – the Maya civilisation began to grow.

Over time, populations grew and were focused around the city-states in the region – Calakmul, Tikal, Copan, Palenque, Coba and Chichen Itza. Soon, some of these cities had huge populations of nearly 100,000 people! Even though we call these people the Maya, each city-state ruled itself individually and was highly competitive; therefore, vicious wars would often erupt between neighbouring city-states.

Looking to the stars

Experts consider ancient Maya astronomy to have been far more accurate than European astronomy: astonishingly, the Maya accurately calculated and measured the length of a year (365.24 days), the length of a lunar month (29.5 days) and they had the ability to predict astronomical events like eclipses.

The mysterious disappearance of the Maya

Despite their technological innovations and organisation, some city-states are believed to have transformed from busy cities to abandoned ruins over the course of just a hundred years!

Archaeologists cannot agree on what happened in the cities. Some say that there was an outbreak of an infectious disease which may have killed much of the population, like Tikal; another group argues that a long drought took place; consequently, not enough fruit, vegetables and cereals could be grown to feed the people.

Do the Maya still exist today?

If a modern-day citizen of Belize were to be asked about their heritage, they would most probably say they were related to the people of Ancient Maya!

It is believed that 60% of the people who live in modern-day Belize are descendants of the Maya. To celebrate the country's heritage and past, Belize's money has Maya symbols printed on it.

Year 6 model text 1: annotated

Dark grey highlights = Words from the National Curriculum word lists

The ancient Maya
↑ heading ────────────→

↓ brief introduction

The ancient Maya were a civilisation that thrived between 2000 BC and AD 1500.

Their city-states spread across Mesoamerica, which is Southern Mexico
↑ technical vocabulary   relative clause ↗
and Central America today. Considered
↖ relative clause
to be extremely advanced for their time, the Maya are still known for their writing, art, science and architecture. Their temples and pyramids can still be found in the jungles of Central America. Strangely, many of the Maya cities were
                                    passive voice ↗
abandoned in the 10th century, which
↖ passive voice
confuses many archaeologists to this day. What could have happened to these powerful city-states?

↓ subheadings

How did the Maya civilisation start to grow?

↓ statements giving factual information
Life was not straightforward during these times, as the Mesoamerican region was not the most forgiving;
                                    semi-colon ↑
although it was fertile, the soil was
↑ subordinating conjunction
not very deep and torrential rainfall washed it away in hilly areas during the rainy season.

In the lowlands, there were only two seasons – rainy or dry. Because of this,

? *Did you know? The Maya built pyramids to get closer to the gods.*

people had to store water to drink and could only grow crops during the rainy season. The Maya invented a genius way to collect and store water for drinking and, in places, to irrigate their
                                    technical vocabulary ↗
farmland – aguadas. These were man-
↖ technical vocabulary
made lakes often lined with lime to prevent the water from seeping through the porous stone below. The Maya
                                    third person ↗
even designed their cities so that water
↖ third person
would drain into the aguada.

With regards to hilly areas, the Maya
↑ conjunctive adverb
constructed terraced farms. This clever
                                    passive voice ↗
technique was used to build farms on
↖ passive voice
steep hills creating a flat surface to grow on, and it stopped the soil from sliding away.

With a plentiful supply of water, crops and an abundance of natural limestone – a natural material used for building –
↑ parenthesis
the Maya civilisation began to grow.

Over time, populations grew and were focused around the city-states in the region – Calakmul, Tikal, Copan, Palenque, Coba and Chichen Itza. Soon, some of these cities had huge populations of nearly 100,000 people! Even though we call these people the Maya, each city-state ruled itself individually and was highly competitive; therefore, vicious wars would often erupt
↑ word ending in -cious
between neighbouring city-states.

Looking to the stars

Experts consider ancient Maya
↑ third person
astronomy to have been far more accurate than European astronomy:
colon ↗
astonishingly, the Maya accurately calculated and measured the length of a year (365.24 days), the length of a lunar month (29.5 days) and
↑ parenthesis
they had the ability to predict astronomical
technical vocabulary ↗
events like eclipses.
↖ technical vocabulary

The mysterious disappearance of the Maya

Despite their technological innovations and organisation, some city-states are believed to have transformed from busy cities to abandoned ruins over the course of just a hundred years!

Archaeologists cannot agree on what
↓ formal language
happened in the cities. Some say that there was an outbreak of an infectious
word ending in -tious ↑
disease which may have killed much
relative clause ↗
of the population, like Tikal; another
↖ relative clause
group argues that a long drought took place; consequently, not enough fruit,
↑ conjunctive adverb
vegetables and cereals could be grown to feed the people.

Do the Maya still exist today?

If a modern-day citizen of Belize were
subjunctive mood/form ↗
to be asked about their heritage, they
↖ subjunctive mood/form
would most probably say they were related to the people of Ancient Maya!

↓→ passive voice
It is believed that 60% of the
↓→ passive voice
people who live in modern-
↓→ passive voice
day Belize are descendants
↓→ passive voice →
of the Maya. To celebrate the country's heritage and
apostrophe for possession ↗
past, Belize's money
↖ apostrophe for possession
has Maya symbols printed on it.

Year 6 model text 2

The Shang Dynasty

Remarkably, evidence of the Shang Dynasty – also historically known as the Yin Dynasty – was not confirmed until 1899, after a scholar recognised the engravings on ancient animal bones.

Further investigation identified these bones as originating from north-east China; however, it was not until 1928 that excavations began and the existence of the Shang Dynasty was confirmed. Although earlier dynasties are referred to in Chinese legend, the Shang Dynasty is the first well-documented era in Chinese history, with numerous written and archaeological sources available to study. Due to this evidence, much more is now known about this era of Chinese history.

Power and Rule

Most historians now date the dynasty from 1600-1046 BC. The area surrounding the Yellow River, which is often referred to as the 'cradle of Chinese civilisation', is thought to be its main location, though the capital was moved around on several occasions. Shang society was divided into different classes. The king held the highest position within the dynasty, with most of the high-level officials being his relatives, who formed the government. Even though the Shang ruled over three thousand years ago, this government is viewed as advanced. Similarly to modern governance, taxes were collected from the citizens to support the empire. Tributes were also paid to the emperor by noble warriors, who were granted land in return for their loyalty. Equally, warlords – who often ruled areas of surrounding land but were loyal to the king – provided soldiers during times of war so that the kingdom could be defended.

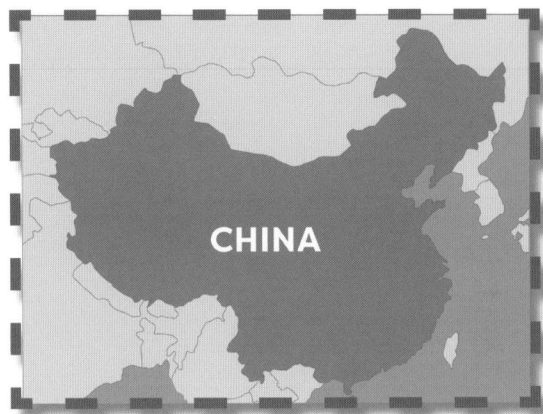

Evidence discovered by archaeologists supports the theory that the king and the nobles lived inside walled cities in palaces and other grand buildings, as this is where remains of precious jade, bone, pottery and bronze work have been located, whereas those from lower down in the social ranking (primarily farmers) lived in wooden houses outside of the city walls or in the countryside.

> **?** *Did you know the first ruler of the Shang Dynasty was Emperor Tang, who was a military leader? In total, there were thirty Shang emperors.*

Farmers

Much of the population living under Shang rule were farmers. Whilst China is well-known for its rice production, these farmers were more likely to have grown millet, wheat and barley as rice was generally farmed in the southern regions. They used the Yellow River's water to create a large irrigation system to supply their crops with water. As well as this, the farmers also kept livestock – sheep, pigs and oxen – to supplement their crop production. Some historians also believe that silkworms were farmed to make silk: an industry that China would become world-famous for after the establishment of the Silk Road in the first century BC.

Inventions

Incredibly, modern Chinese writing has evolved directly from the early written symbols developed during the Shang period. In fact, the Shang were the first known Chinese rulers to promote the use of writing which they used to record their history; hence, there is a greater level of understanding about this era. In addition, the rulers understood that writing could enable them to lead a more organised society and government: it made the formation of a bureaucracy possible.

Some of these written symbols were also discovered incised onto oracle bones (tortoise shells or oxen bones), many of which were found during archaeological excavations.

Clearly, the Shang Dynasty was an era of great importance, especially in terms of their advancements in communication and technology which have inspired items that have been used throughout history. Despite its great success, its power could not last forever: evidence suggests that the Shang Dynasty came to an end when it was succeeded by the Zhou Dynasty.

Year 6 model text 2: annotated

Dark grey highlights = Words from the National Curriculum word lists

The Shang Dynasty

↑ heading

Remarkably, evidence of the Shang
↑ brief introduction
Dynasty – also historically known as the

Yin Dynasty – was not confirmed until
passive voice ↗
1899, after a scholar recognised the
↖ passive voice
engravings on ancient animal bones.

Further investigation identified these

bones as originating from north-east
↓ conjunctive adverb
China; however, it was not until 1928
↑ semi-colon
that excavations began and the

existence of the Shang Dynasty was

confirmed. Although earlier dynasties

are referred to in Chinese legend,

the Shang Dynasty is the first well-
statement giving factual information ↗
documented era in Chinese history, with
↖ statement giving factual information
numerous written and archaeological

sources available to study. Due to this

evidence, much more is now known

about this era of Chinese history.

↓ subheading
Power and Rule

Most historians now date the dynasty
↑ third person
from 1600-1046 BC. The area surrounding

the Yellow River, which is often referred
relative clause ↗
to as the 'cradle of Chinese civilisation', is
↖ relative clause
thought to be its main location, though

the capital was moved around on several

occasions. Shang society was divided

into different classes. The king held the

highest position within the dynasty,

CHINA

with most of the high-level officials

being his relatives, who formed the

government. Even though the Shang

ruled over three thousand years ago,

this government is viewed as advanced.

Similarly to modern governance, taxes
↑ conjunctive adverb   ↑ technical vocabulary
were collected from the citizens to

support the empire. Tributes were also
passive voice ↗
paid to the emperor by noble warriors,
↖ passive voice
who were granted land in return for
↖ passive voice   ↓ conjunctive adverb
their loyalty. Equally, warlords – who
↖ passive voice   dashes for parenthesis ↗
often ruled areas of surrounding land
↖ dashes for parenthesis
but were loyal to the king – provided
↖ dashes for parenthesis
soldiers during times of war so that the
subordinating conjunction ↑
kingdom could be defended.

Evidence discovered by archaeologists
formal language ↗
supports the theory that the king and
↖ formal language
the nobles lived inside walled cities in

palaces and other grand buildings, as

this is where remains of precious jade,

bone, pottery and bronze work have
been located, whereas those from lower
down in the social ranking (primarily

brackets for parenthesis ↗

farmers) lived in wooden houses outside

↖ brackets for parenthesis

of the city walls or in the countryside.

? **Did you know the first
ruler of the Shang
Dynasty was Emperor Tang,
who was a military leader?
In total, there were thirty
Shang emperors.**

Farmers

Much of the population living under
Shang rule were farmers. Whilst China is
well-known for its rice production, these
farmers were more likely to have grown
millet, wheat and barley as rice was
generally farmed in the southern regions.
They used the Yellow River's water to

↑ past tense   *apostrophe for possession ↑*

create a large irrigation system to supply
their crops with water. As well as this,

conjunctive adverb ↑

the farmers also kept livestock – sheep,

↑ past tense   *dashes for parenthesis ↗*

pigs and oxen – to supplement their crop

↖ dashes for parenthesis   *formal language ↗*

production. Some historians also believe

↖ formal language

that silkworms were farmed to make silk:

↑ passive voice   *colon ↑*

an industry that China would become
world-famous for after the establishment
of the Silk Road in the first century BC.

Inventions

Incredibly, modern Chinese writing has
evolved directly from the early written
symbols developed during the Shang
period. In fact, the Shang were the

statement giving factual information ↗

first known Chinese rulers to promote

↖↓ statement giving factual information

the use of writing which they used to

↖↓ statement giving factual information

record their history; hence, there is a

↑ conjunctive adverb

greater level of understanding about
this era. In addition, the rulers

↑ conjunctive adverb

understood that writing could enable
them to lead a more organised society
and government: it made the formation

colon ↑   *technical vocabulary ↗*

of a bureaucracy possible.

↖ technical vocabulary

Some of these written symbols were

passive voice ↗

also discovered incised onto oracle

↖ passive voice

bones (tortoise shells or oxen bones),

↑ brackets for parenthesis

many of which were found during

↑ passive voice

archaeological excavations.

Clearly, the Shang Dynasty was an

↑ third person

era of great importance, especially
in terms of their advancements in
communication and technology
which have inspired items that have
been used throughout history. Despite
its great success, its power could not
last forever: evidence suggests that

colon ↑

the Shang Dynasty came to an
end when it was succeeded

↑ subordinating conjunction

by the Zhou Dynasty.

Recounts: diary entries

The purpose of a diary entry is to share a personal account of an event.

Tips for children to write diary recount texts

🐾 Children can find it easier to write about their real-life experiences. When possible, consider how you could enable children to see or experience what they are going to write a diary entry about. For example, could they visit the seaside or a park before writing about these places?

🐾 The use of role play can be really effective when teaching children about this text type. Ask an adult to dress up as the character you are going to invite the children to write about, for example, Charles Darwin. Then let the children ask questions about an event in that character's life. You could prompt them with a question like, 'Did you ever meet Alfred Wallace?' The children can take notes based on the interview before writing a diary entry in role as that character.

🐾 Recounts don't always have to be long. Think about ways that people recount what they've done, other than by writing diaries. Postcards are a great way for children to write shorter recounts as they still require children to use the key features of a recount, including writing in the past tense and in the first person.

Consider providing photographs to remind children of the events that they are going to write about. For younger or less confident writers, you could ask them to order the pictures you provide, before writing a sentence about what happened in chronological order.

Teach the children to show the emotion of the writer rather than describing it. For example, instead of 'I was scared...' share alternatives which suit the event like 'my fingers trembled' or 'my heart pounded'. This is an effective way to support children in developing inference skills as readers, too.

For older and more confident writers, consider how a narrator's attitude and personality can be shown in writing.

Note that if children are writing a historical recount text, their language choices and word order might be different to a modern-day recount. For example, ask the children what might be different if they were writing from the perspective of a Victorian child?

'Working at greater depth' explained

There are two texts for Year 6 level in this chapter. The second Year 6 text on pages 126 – 129 is designed to show 'greater depth'.

- This diary entry contains a mixture of factual information and the author's own viewpoint about the events, with regular references to how the character is feeling: 'I must admit that I wished he had not suggested such an idea!'

- Rhetorical questions are used: 'Had they been captured?'

- A more old-fashioned tone and old-fashioned, formal language have been used to make the text feel appropriate to the time it is describing (the 19th century). For example, 'My apprehension was unfounded' (as opposed to 'I shouldn't have been worried').

- Technical language related to the sea and ships has been selected to make the account feel more authentic: 'skipper', 'captain', 'starboard', 'port', 'deck' and 'cabin'.

- Higher-level punctuation is used throughout.

Year 3 overview

Use this overview and the checklist alongside the Year 3 model text (pages 104 – 107).

🐾 Specific features for this text type

• Dates – say when the account was written	
• Salutation (optional)	*Dear Diary...*
• Chronological order – sequenced paragraphs	*this afternoon, yesterday at 2:00 am, two weeks ago*
• Past tense	*felt, heard, touched*
• First person – informal	*I took a deep breath and closed my eyes.*
• A mixture of facts and opinions	
• Rhetorical questions	*Can you believe it?*
• Sign off (optional)	

The following lists should be used as a tool to help teachers plan where to cover explicit grammar, punctuation and spelling objectives from both the Teacher Assessment Framework and the National Curriculum Programmes of Study.

🐾 Grammar

• Coordinating conjunctions – link ideas with 'but', 'so', 'and' or 'for'	*I couldn't say the dog had eaten my homework again so I had to come up with a more realistic excuse.*
• Subordinating conjunctions – expand upon independent clauses with 'when', 'whilst', 'before' or 'after'	*After Benji helped James to score the goal, I felt like a complete loser.*
• Adverbs / adverbials of time – say when events took place	*Once the school bell had rung... When I got back from the match...*
• Adverbs / adverbials of place – say where events took place	*in Mr Jones' chemistry class*
• Expanded noun phrases – add detail to nouns	*the whole school the boy down the street*

🐾 Punctuation

- Apostrophes for omission   *couldn't, wouldn't, shouldn't*
- Apostrophes for possession   *the coach's idea...*
- Exclamation marks   *It's totally unfair!*

🐾 Spelling

- Year 3 / 4 words from the National Curriculum word lists: see page 9 of this book for a list of these. These words are highlighted in the Year 3 model text.

🐾 Checklist

Use this checklist with the Year 3 model text. See page 7 for more information.

Dates	
Salutation	
Chronological order	
Past tense	
First person	
Facts and opinions	
Rhetorical questions	
Sign off	
Grammar: Coordinating conjunctions	
Grammar: Subordinating conjunctions	
Grammar: Adverbs / adverbials of time	
Grammar: Adverbs / adverbials of place	
Grammar: Expanded noun phrases	
Punctuation: Apostrophes for omission	
Punctuation: Apostrophes for possession	
Punctuation: Exclamation marks	
Spelling: Year 3 / 4 word list	

Year 3 model text

January 61 AD

My name is Queen Boudicca and this is my story.

As Queen of the Iceni, I ruled a territory that will come to be known as East Anglia, alongside my husband, King Prasutagus. He is dead now, but before he died, he declared that half of our kingdom should belong to me and the other half to the Roman Emperor, Nero.

Did those barbaric Romans keep to this deal? Of course they didn't! Instead, they increased our taxes, took away our land and farms and publically flogged me. I wouldn't stand for this, so I decided to fight back!

When the Roman governor, Suetonius, was away, I decided to strike! Camulodunum was to be my target. I waited until he was busy elsewhere to attack so that I had the greatest chance of success. In 60 AD, I ordered my warriors, both women and men, to attack the Roman town, slaughter any enemies that they saw and set fire to the houses and buildings there. I even ordered them to burn the town's temple, for I knew there were some Romans sheltered there.

After we had easily destroyed the town, I turned my attention southwards and continued with my forces, ransacking both Londinium and Verulamium. Was this my chance to finally regain power and drive the Romans from our lands for good?

That night, when Suetonius heard the terrible news, he rallied more troops and headed towards my trail of destruction. Confident in our abilities, I sent for our families to come and watch us defeat the monstrous Romans because I had many more men than Suetonius did. This was a huge mistake.

Finally, our troops met on a battlefield near Shropshire. I was foolish to believe my troops would be enough to match the well-trained and experienced Romans. We attacked bravely, but the Romans countered and they drove my warriors back with their greater discipline, better armour and weaponry. Before we could muster up the strength to fight back, my army was destroyed. We had lost! I had to admit defeat.

Desperation filled my body as I realised I would be captured and taken to Rome to be punished. This couldn't happen. I wouldn't allow it so I decided to end my life.

Boudicca

Year 3 model text: annotated

Dark grey highlights = Words from the National Curriculum word lists

January 61 AD
↑ date

My name is Queen Boudicca and this is my story.
↑ salutation

As Queen of the Iceni, I ruled a territory that will come to be known as
↑ first person   ↓→ fact
East Anglia, alongside my husband, King Prasutagus. He is dead now,
↓→ fact
but before he died, he declared that half of our kingdom should belong
coordinating ↗
conjunction   ↓→ fact
to me and the other half to the Roman Emperor, Nero.

exclamation mark ↓
Did those barbaric Romans keep to this deal? Of course they didn't!
↑ rhetorical question   apostrophe for omission ↑
Instead, they increased our taxes, took away our land and farms and

publically flogged me. I wouldn't stand for this, so I decided to fight back!
coordinating conjunction ↗

When the Roman governor, Suetonius, was away, I decided to strike!
↑ subordinating conjunction   past tense ↗
Camulodunum was to be my target. I waited until he was busy

elsewhere to attack so that I had the greatest chance of success.
↑ expanded noun phrase
In 60 AD, I ordered my warriors, both women and men, to attack the
↑ adverbial of time
Roman town, slaughter any enemies that they saw and set fire to the

houses and buildings there. I even ordered them to burn the town's
apostrophe for possession ↗
temple, for I knew there were some Romans sheltered there.
↑ coordinating conjunction

After we had easily destroyed
↑ subordinating conjunction
the town, I turned my attention
↑ first person
southwards and continued with my
↑ coordinating conjunction
forces, ransacking both Londinium

and Verulamium. Was this my chance

to finally regain power and drive the

Romans from our lands for good?
↑ adverbial of place

That night, when Suetonius heard
↑ adverbial of time
the terrible news, he rallied more
↑ opinion
troops and headed towards my

trail of destruction. Confident in

our abilities, I sent for our families

to come and watch us defeat the monstrous Romans because I had
↑ expanded noun phrase
many more men than Suetonius did. This was a huge mistake.
↑ opinion

↓ chronological order   ↓ fact
Finally, our troops met on a battlefield near Shropshire. I was foolish
↑ adverb of time   ↑ opinion
to believe my troops would be enough to match the well-trained
                                                    expanded noun phrase ↗
and experienced Romans. We attacked bravely, but the Romans
↖ expanded noun phrase
countered and they drove my warriors back with their greater

discipline, better armour and weaponry. Before we could muster up

the strength to fight back, my army was destroyed. We had lost!

I had to admit defeat.

Desperation filled my body as I realised I would be captured and

taken to Rome to be punished. This couldn't happen. I wouldn't

allow it so I decided to end my life.
↑ coordinating conjunction

Boudicca
↑ sign off

Year 4 overview

Use this overview and the checklist alongside the Year 4 model text (pages 110 – 113).

🦖 Specific features for this text type

• Dates – say when the account was written	
• Salutation (optional)	
• Chronological order – sequenced paragraphs	*a couple of days ago, yesterday evening, previously*
• Past tense	*realised, discovered, understood*
• First person – informal language	*Before I could work out what was happening...*
• A mixture of facts and opinions	
• Rhetorical questions	*How long will I have to stay here?*
• Sign off (optional)	

The following lists should be used as a tool to help teachers plan where to cover explicit grammar, punctuation and spelling objectives from both the Teacher Assessment Framework and the National Curriculum Programmes of Study.

🦖 Grammar

• Coordinating conjunctions – link ideas with 'but', 'so', 'and' or 'for'	*I followed my sister into the cottage and suddenly realised the old woman's sinister plan.*
• Subordinating conjunctions – expand upon independent clauses with 'when', 'whilst', 'before' or 'after'	*Before I had chance to escape, a chain had been clamped to my leg.*
• Adverbs / adverbials of time – say when events took place	*Without warning, the witch...*
• Adverbs / adverbials of place – say where events took place	*in the midst of the dark forest, along the trail*
• Expanded noun phrases – add detail to nouns	*the majestic, tall trees*

🐾 Punctuation

- Commas for fronted adverbials   *Once she had left the room, I huddled closer...*
- Apostrophes for omission   *shouldn't, can't, won't, aren't*
- Apostrophes for possession   *the witch's icy grasp, the cottage's chimney*

🐾 Spelling

- Year 3 / 4 words from the National Curriculum word lists: see page 9 of this book for a list of these. These words are highlighted in the Year 4 model text.

🐾 Checklist

Use this checklist with the Year 4 model text. See page 7 for more information.

Dates	
Salutation	
Chronological order	
Past tense	
First person	
Facts and opinions	
Rhetorical questions	
Sign off	
Grammar: Coordinating conjunctions	
Grammar: Subordinating conjunctions	
Grammar: Adverbs / adverbials of time	
Grammar: Adverbs / adverbials of place	
Grammar: Expanded noun phrases	
Punctuation: Commas for fronted adverbials	
Punctuation: Apostrophes for omission	
Punctuation: Apostrophes for possession	
Spelling: Year 3 / 4 word list	

Year 4 model text

January 793 AD

Dear diary,

Last night, horror struck our Holy Island of Lindisfarne! The same Viking men had returned – I remembered them. They came ashore on long, wooden ships. They wielded round shields and weapons – mostly axes. They screamed. They shouted. None of us could understand their demands or questions. My holy brother, Wulfstan, stepped forward to greet the men, but one of the strange-looking foreigners grabbed his arm and threw him to the ground. Without letting go, the brute slowly turned his axe to each of the ten of us gathered round and spoke calmly.

Horror struck my eyes – in one fell swoop, he had chopped brother Wulfstan's arm clean off! Screams erupted all around me as the group of men began to attack us. Without hesitation, I darted towards the priory to take shelter. With each step, clanks of iron and ruptures of pain-filled screams exploded behind me.

At first, I thought I had found shelter within the walls of the priory. The door was firmly closed and bolted. Breathing heavily, I pushed all my weight up against the wooden door to stop them entering. After a few moments, a ribbon of black smoke snaked its way up from underneath the door. I watched nervously as it slithered up towards the ceiling. The invaders had set the priory alight!

Without hesitation, I scrambled over to the back entrance of the building and looked worriedly back towards the suffocated entrance to my beloved home. Tears and smoke blurred my vision as my eyes fell upon all the history contained in the building. The memories! The treasures! The gold crosses, silver goblets and the resting place of our sacred St Cuthbert.

I couldn't believe my eyes – all would be lost.

Slowly but surely, they were breaking the door down, so I left my brothers behind. I escaped through the back door and made off towards the hills in hope of finding a place to take refuge. What I saw when I looked back will never be forgotten.

Curse these Viking raiders! When will this madness end?

Aethbert

Year 4 model text: annotated

Dark grey highlights = Words from the National Curriculum word lists

January 793 AD
↑ date

Dear diary,
↑ salutation

Last night, horror struck our Holy Island of Lindisfarne! The same Viking
↑ adverbial of time

men had returned – I remembered them. They came ashore on long,
                                                              facts ↗

wooden ships. They wielded round shields and weapons – mostly axes.
↖ facts

They screamed. They shouted. None of us could understand their
↑ past tense

demands or questions. My holy brother, Wulfstan, stepped forward to

greet the men, but one of the strange-looking foreigners grabbed his

coordinating conjunction ↗   ↑ opinion

arm and threw him to the ground. Without letting go, the brute slowly

turned his axe to each of the ten of us gathered round and spoke calmly.

Horror struck my eyes – in one fell swoop, he had chopped brother

Wulfstan's arm clean off! Screams erupted all around me as the group
↑ apostrophe for possession   ↑ adverbial of place

of men began to attack us. Without hesitation, I darted towards the

                                                     adverbial of place ↗

priory to take shelter. With each step, clanks of iron and ruptures of
↖ adverbial of place   ↑ expanded noun phrase

pain-filled screams exploded behind me.

At first, I thought I had found shelter within the walls
          ↑ comma for fronted adverbial
of the priory. The door was firmly closed and bolted.

Breathing heavily, I pushed all my weight up against

the wooden door to stop them entering. After a few

moments, a ribbon of black smoke snaked its way up from underneath
↑ expanded noun phrase   adverbial of place ↗
the door. I watched nervously as it slithered up towards the ceiling.
↖ adverbial of place
The invaders had set the priory alight!

Without hesitation, I scrambled over to the back
↖ comma for fronted adverbial
entrance of the building and looked worriedly

back towards the suffocated entrance to my
expanded noun phrase ↗
beloved home. Tears and smoke blurred my
↖ expanded noun phrase   first person ↗
vision as my eyes fell upon all the history contained in the building.

The memories! The treasures! The gold crosses, silver goblets and the

resting place of our sacred St Cuthbert.

I couldn't believe my eyes – all would be lost.
↑ apostrophe for omission

Slowly but surely, they were breaking the door down, so I left my brothers
↖ comma for fronted adverbial   ↖ coordinating conjunction
behind. I escaped through the back door and made off towards the hills

in hope of finding a place to take refuge. What I saw when I looked back
                       first person ↗   ↑ subordinating conjunction
will never be forgotten.

Curse these Viking raiders! When will this madness end?
                        ↑ rhetorical question

Aethbert
↑ sign off

Year 5 overview

Use this overview and the checklist alongside the Year 5 model text (pages 116 – 119).

🐾 Specific features for this text type

- Dates – say when the account was written
- Salutation / sign off (optional)
- Chronological order – sequenced paragraphs
- Past tense — *Before I opened the door, I stopped to think.*
- First person – informal language — *We couldn't believe what was happening to us.*
- A mixture of facts and opinions
- Rhetorical questions — *What was lurking behind that door?*

The following lists should be used as a tool to help teachers plan where to cover explicit grammar, punctuation and spelling objectives from both the Teacher Assessment Framework and the National Curriculum Programmes of Study.

🐾 Grammar

- Subordinating conjunctions – expand upon independent clauses with 'when', 'whilst', 'before' or 'after' — *When Lady Beatrice got up to investigate, a deathly silence descended upon us.*
- Conjunctive adverbs – flow from one point to another
  - Opposite points — *The door had been locked before we retired to our quarters; despite this, the door was now wide open.*
  - Emphasis — *Of course, we needed to come up with a plan.*
- Relative clauses – embed extra information — *The manor, which was suffocated in a thick ivy, stood atop a barren moor.*
- Adverbs / adverbials of time – say when events took place — *As the clock struck midnight...*
- Adverbs / adverbials of place – say where events took place — *across the desolate moor surrounding the manor*
- Expanded noun phrases – add detail to nouns — *icy fingers with sharp nails*

🐾 Punctuation

- Commas for parenthesis   *Baron Foxhouse, who had visited the manor twice before, insisted that...*

🐾 Spelling

- Year 5 / 6 words from the National Curriculum word lists: see page 9 of this book for a list of these. These words are highlighted in the Year 5 model text.

🐾 Checklist

Use this checklist with the Year 5 model text. See page 7 for more information.

Dates	
Salutation / sign off (optional)	
Chronological order	
Past tense	
First person	
Facts and opinions	
Rhetorical questions	
Grammar: Subordinating conjunctions	
Grammar: Conjunctive adverbs	
Grammar: Relative clauses	
Grammar: Adverbs / adverbials of time	
Grammar: Adverbs / adverbials of place	
Grammar: Expanded noun phrases	
Punctuation: Commas for parenthesis	
Spelling: Year 5 / 6 word list	

Year 5 model text

The discovery of Tutankhamun's tomb

Sunday 26th November 1922

Today has been the most excellent of days! Our discoveries have finally led us to the inner chamber of the tomb where the Egyptian pharaoh Tutankhamun was buried.

On Friday, we were able to completely reveal a sealed doorway, which was covered in a variety of symbols showing Tutankhamun's name. Upon closer inspection, I discovered that the doorway had been opened and resealed before our discovery. We were most surprised! In the staircase entrance, there were piles of rubbish including broken pots, boxes of possessions with other pharaohs' names on them and even a scarab. Disappointed, we thought that the only explanation for this was that the tomb had probably been opened before by tomb robbers, who were intent on plundering the precious artefacts. A disastrous end to our hard work... Or so we thought!

After clearing almost nine metres of nuisance items from the passageway, we came across a second, sealed doorway, which was almost exactly the same as the first. Immediately, we cleared away any of the remaining bits of rubbish which were blocking our way until only the sealed doorway was in front of us! Was this the moment we had been waiting for? Were we on the brink of an incredible discovery?

Carefully, so that I didn't disturb the tomb or interfere with the structure more than was necessary, I made a tiny hole in the top left corner of the doorway, where I hoped to see what was beyond it. It was clear from our testing that there was an empty space behind the doorway.

Every muscle in my body tightened as I quickly attempted to widen the hole a little more whilst Lord Carnarvon and Lady Herbert waited impatiently behind me. Inside, I was able to see the interior of the chamber, which was filled with a great range of extraordinary and beautiful objects. They were right in front of me and were heaped in great piles!

Straight away, I exclaimed to my companions about the marvellous sight in front of me. Before we could explore the artefacts further, we required the light from both a torch and an additional candle so that we could be sure of what we had seen. I was conscious of the fact that our hopes had been raised in the past and did not want to repeat that experience. It is difficult to describe the sensation of wonder and astonishment that kidnapped our senses at that moment; however, I can honestly say that I felt utterly overjoyed!

Through the gap, we could see the most incredible things: decorated couches, exquisitely-painted boxes, models of a king, golden chariots and more! Our eyes couldn't take it all in! Was this a tomb or merely a store for the pharaoh's possessions? Surely, it must be his tomb! What other explanation could there be?

Confused, we searched for answers until we noticed another sealed doorway, which was between the two statues. Additionally, this doorway bore the sign of numerous cartouches bearing the name of Tutankhamun. This proved, with little doubt, that we had finally discovered the tomb we had been searching for!

Year 5 model text: annotated

Dark grey highlights = Words from the National Curriculum word lists

The discovery of Tutankhamun's tomb

↓ date
Sunday 26th November 1922

Today has been the most excellent of days! Our discoveries have finally
fact ↗
led us to the inner chamber of the tomb where the Egyptian pharaoh
↖ fact
Tutankhamun was buried.
↖ fact

↓ first person
On Friday, we were able to completely reveal a sealed doorway, which
↑ chronological order ↓↗   relative clause ↗
was covered in a variety of symbols showing Tutankhamun's name. Upon
↖ relative clause
closer inspection, I discovered that the doorway had been opened and
resealed before our discovery. We were most surprised! In the staircase
                                                        ↑ adverbial of place
entrance, there were piles of rubbish including broken pots, boxes of
                                                        expanded noun phrase ↗
possessions with other pharaohs' names on them and even a scarab.
↖ expanded noun phrase
Disappointed, we thought that the only explanation for this was that the
tomb had probably been opened before by tomb robbers, who were intent
                                                        relative clause ↗
on plundering the precious artefacts. A disastrous end to our hard work...
↖ relative clause
Or so we thought!

After clearing almost nine metres of nuisance items from the passageway,
we came across a second, sealed doorway, which was almost exactly the
                                                        past tense ↗
same as the first. Immediately, we cleared away any of the remaining bits
↖ past tense   ↑ adverb of time
of rubbish which were blocking our way until only the sealed doorway was
in front of us! Was this the moment we had been waiting for? Were
                                                        rhetorical questions ↗
we on the brink of an incredible discovery?
↖ rhetorical questions

Carefully, so that I didn't disturb the tomb or interfere with the structure
                                                        commas for parenthesis ↗
more than was necessary, I made a tiny hole in the top left corner of
↖ commas for parenthesis   expanded noun phrase ↗
the doorway, where I hoped to see what was beyond it. It was clear
↖ expanded noun phrase
from our testing that there was an empty space behind the doorway.
                                                        ↑ adverbial of place

Grammarsaurus KS2© Mitch Hudson and Anna Richards 2021

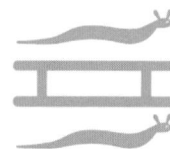

Every muscle in my body tightened as I quickly

attempted to widen the hole a little more

whilst Lord Carnarvon and Lady Herbert
↑ subordinating conjunction
waited impatiently behind me. Inside,
↑ opinion
I was able to see the interior of the
                       expanded noun phrase ↗
chamber, which was filled with a great
↖ expanded noun phrase
range of extraordinary and beautiful

objects. They were right in front of me
                       ↑ adverbial of place
and were heaped in great piles!

Straight away, I exclaimed to my
↑ adverbial of time   ↑ first person
companions about the marvellous sight in

front of me. Before we could explore the artefacts further, we required
       ↑ subordinating conjunction   fact ↗
the light from both a torch and an additional candle so that we could
↖ fact
be sure of what we had seen. I was conscious of the fact that our hopes

had been raised in the past and did not want to repeat that experience.

It is difficult to describe the sensation of wonder and astonishment that

kidnapped our senses at that moment; however, I can honestly say that
                                    ↑ conjunctive adverb   opinion ↗
I felt utterly overjoyed!
↖ opinion

Through the gap, we could see the most incredible things: decorated
↑ adverbial of place   ↑ opinion
couches, exquisitely-painted boxes, models of a king, golden chariots
              ↑ expanded noun phrase
and more! Our eyes couldn't take it all in! Was this a tomb or merely

a store for the pharaoh's possessions? Surely, it must be his tomb!
↑ expanded noun phrase   ↑ conjunctive adverb
What other explanation could there be?
↑ rhetorical question

Confused, we searched for answers until we noticed another sealed
       ↑ past tense
doorway, which was between the two statues. Additionally, this
                                          ↑ conjunctive adverb
doorway bore the sign of numerous cartouches bearing the name

of Tutankhamun. This proved, with little doubt, that we had finally
                           ↑ commas for parenthesis
discovered the tomb we had been searching for!

Year 6 overview

Use this overview and the checklist alongside the Year 6 model texts (pages 122 – 129).

🐾 Specific features for this text type

- Dates – say when the account was written
- Salutation / sign off (optional)
- Chronological order – sequenced paragraphs
- Past tense — *I didn't have to think twice; I said 'yes' straight away.*
- First person – informal language — *We discovered something amazing.*
- A mixture of facts and opinions
- Rhetorical questions — *Where could our adventure take us next?*

The following lists should be used as a tool to help teachers plan where to cover explicit grammar, punctuation and spelling objectives from both the Teacher Assessment Framework and the National Curriculum Programmes of Study.

🐾 Grammar

- Subjunctive mood/form — *Star Command HQ insisted that we be present for the debrief.*
- Subordinating conjunctions – expand upon independent clauses with 'when', 'whilst', 'before' or 'after' — *After I had found out about the mission, I couldn't wait to get started.*
- Conjunctive adverbs – flow from one point to another
  - Additional points — *...a thick poison covered the planet. In addition to this, the alien inhabitants were known to be quite aggressive.*
  - Opposite points — *Our enemies shot their ion-powered weapons; however, I knew the blast shields on board would protect us.*
  - Results — *...would take a total of seven months; as a result, members of the crew sleep in cryochambers...*
- Relative clauses – embed extra information — *Planet Arachnid, which orbits the Xen 249 Star, has been sending out emergency signals.*
- Adverbs / adverbials of time — *As the dark day turned into a dark night...*
- Adverbs / adverbials of place — *across the celestial highway*
- Expanded noun phrases – add detail to nouns — *the energy field of the vessel*

🐾 Punctuation

• Semi-colons	*The journey was meant to last seven months; in reality, it took one year.*
• Colons	*The alarm sounded: it was time.*
• Commas, dashes and brackets for parentheses	*The craft, which could comfortably seat up to four passengers, was finally ready...*

🐾 Spelling

- Year 5 / 6 words from the National Curriculum word lists: see page 9 of this book for a list of these. These words are highlighted in the Year 6 model texts.

• Hyphenated words	*well-known, out-of-this-world*

🐾 Checklist

Use this checklist with the Year 6 model texts. See page 7 for more information.

Dates	
Salutation / sign off (optional)	
Chronological order	
Past tense	
First person	
Facts and opinions	
Rhetorical questions	
Grammar: Subjunctive mood/form	
Grammar: Subordinating conjunctions	
Grammar: Conjunctive adverbs	
Grammar: Relative clauses	
Grammar: Adverbs / adverbials of time / place	
Grammar: Expanded noun phrases	
Punctuation: Semi-colons / colons	
Punctuation: Commas, dashes and brackets for parentheses	
Spelling: Year 5 / 6 word list	
Spelling: Hyphenated words	

Year 6 model text 1

Darwin's Diary: The Galápagos Islands

September 15th 1835

After four years of travelling aboard Captain Robert Fitzroy's ship – the HMS Beagle – we arrived at the Galápagos Islands, which are located just off the west coast of South America. Unfortunately, the Beagle was too large to land. The captain insisted that we use smaller boats in order to gain access to the smaller islands, where we hoped to study the endemic wildlife in further detail.

September 28th 1835

It is true that the Galápagos Islands have proved to be most intriguing, and I am growing even more curious about the marvellous animals that reside here.

Whilst on the island, I was diligently collecting as many specimens of fauna and flora as was possible when I came across a tortoise. I found it fascinating when someone living on the island told me that the size of these creatures varied from island to island. Now, we had seen giant tortoises on another island and the crew had even taken the opportunity to capture several of these for their dinner! I can't imagine eating a tortoise! I must admit that I could not be persuaded into partaking in this delicacy!

October 17th 1835

After a frustrating few weeks, with adverse weather proving to be a hindrance, we were prevented from landing on Abingdon Island. However, we were not to be disheartened and travelled to Santiago Island, where we hoped to be able to restock our fresh water supplies. This was not possible but the ship's physician – Benjamin Bynoe – and I remained behind to investigate.

During this week, we have been able explore and record even more specimens: fish, snails, several varieties of bird, reptiles and some insects. Nevertheless, it was interesting to note that there were surprisingly few insects to be found here. Moreover, whilst I've been upon these islands, I have made the most startling discovery!

Incredibly, although the creatures found on the different islands are similar, they are all perfectly adapted to their specific environments. I wondered how this had happened. Among those creatures which struck me the most were the finches, which are small birds that inhabit most of the islands.

24th September 1859

My observations on the islands all those years ago showed that the finches living on each individual island all had distinct beak shapes; apart from that, they had the same short tails, bodies and plumage. You could be mistaken for thinking they were the same unless you observed their beaks more closely. I found that all the beaks were slightly different sizes. The shape varies too, with one sub-group's beaks looking slightly parrot-shaped, whilst another group's beaks are more similar to the beaks one might find on a starling.

Hence the only explanation which can be offered is that after spending long intervals of time in isolated places – and after having to compete with other animals living there – the different species have adapted to survive. Furthermore, this modification can also be identified in their descendants, which have adapted to suit the varied habitats that they occupy.

All of this will be included in my book, but how will the world react to my findings? Will my theory of evolution provoke controversy?

Year 6 model text 1: annotated

Dark grey highlights = Words from the National Curriculum word lists

Darwin's Diary: The Galápagos Islands

September 15th 1835
↑ chronological order

After four years of travelling aboard Captain Robert Fitzroy's ship – the HMS
dashes for parenthesis ↗
Beagle – we arrived at the Galápagos Islands, which are located just off the
↖ dashes for parenthesis
west coast of South America. Unfortunately, the Beagle was too large to land.
facts ↗
The captain insisted that we use smaller boats in order to gain access to the
↖ facts   ↑ subjunctive mood/form   facts ↗
smaller islands, where we hoped to study the endemic wildlife in further detail.
↖ facts   ↑ relative clause

September 28th 1835
↑ dates

It is true that the Galápagos Islands have proved to be most intriguing, and I

am growing even more curious about the marvellous animals that reside here.

↓→ past tense ─────────────────────────────→
Whilst on the island, I was diligently collecting as many specimens of fauna
↓→ past tense ──────────────────────────→
and flora as was possible when I came across a tortoise. I found it fascinating
↑ subordinating conjunction   ↑ first person
when someone living on the island told me that the size of these creatures

varied from island to island. Now, we had seen giant tortoises on another
adverbial of place ↗
island and the crew had even taken the opportunity to capture several of
↖ adverbial of place
these for their dinner! I can't imagine eating a tortoise! I must admit that
↑ opinion
I could not be persuaded into partaking in this delicacy!

October 17th 1835

After a frustrating few weeks, with adverse weather proving to be a
↑ adverbial of time
hindrance, we were prevented from landing on Abingdon Island. However,
↑ first person   ↑ conjunctive adverb
we were not to be disheartened and travelled to Santiago Island, where we
↑ past tense   ↓→ relative clause
hoped to be able to restock our fresh water supplies. This was not possible but
↖↑ relative clause ──────────────────────────────→
the ship's physician – Benjamin Bynoe – and I remained behind to investigate.
↑ dashes for parenthesis

During this week, we have been able explore and record even more
↑ adverbial of time
specimens: fish, snails, several varieties of bird, reptiles and some insects.
↑ colon
Nevertheless, it was interesting to note that there were surprisingly few
↑ conjunctive adverb
insects to be found here. Moreover, whilst I've been upon these islands, I
conjunctive adverb ↑   ↑ subordinating conjunction
have made the most startling discovery!
↖ expanded noun phrase

Incredibly, although the creatures found on the different islands are similar,
↑ subordinating conjunction   ↑ adverbial of place
they are all perfectly adapted to their specific environments. I wondered

how this had happened. Among those creatures which struck me the most

were the finches, which are small birds that inhabit most of the islands.
↑ relative clause

24th September 1859

My observations on the islands all those years ago showed that the
expanded noun phrase ↗
finches living on each individual island all had distinct beak shapes; apart
↖ expanded noun phrase   semi-colon ↑
from that, they had the same short tails, bodies and plumage. You could be

mistaken for thinking they were the same unless you observed their beaks

more closely. I found that all the beaks were slightly different sizes. The
↑ first person
shape varies too, with one sub-group's beaks looking slightly parrot-shaped,
↑ hyphenated word   ↑ hyphenated word
whilst another group's beaks are more similar to the beaks one might find
↑ subordinating conjunction
on a starling.

Hence the only explanation which can be offered is that after spending
↑ conjunctive adverb
long intervals of time in isolated places – and after having to compete with
dashes for parenthesis ↗
other animals living there – the different species have adapted to survive.
↖ dashes for parenthesis   ↑ fact
Furthermore, this modification can also be identified in their descendants,
↑ conjunctive adverb
which have adapted to suit the varied habitats that they occupy.
↑ relative clause

↑→ rhetorical questions
All of this will be included in my book, but how will the world
↓ rhetorical questions
react to my findings? Will my theory of evolution provoke

controversy?

Year 6 model text 2

The mystery of the Mary Celeste

12th December 1872

What happened today was the strangest thing I have ever seen – or will ever see – which is why I feel most obliged to record my faithful account of the curious event. Perhaps, one day, someone shall read my hurried notes about the mystery surrounding the Mary Celeste.

From my position in the crow's nest, where I had been keeping watch, my eyes were drawn eastwards: dawn was fast approaching, which would signal the end of my duty. Suddenly, emerging out of the early morning mist, I could just about make out the vague outline of a ship. Now, this in itself is not unusual. Initially, my first thought was that it was a cargo ship which was returning westwards: such ships carrying goods like wine and clothes were familiar sights. However, upon closer inspection (and to my utter incredulity), I was made to realise that it was out of control.

As the seconds raced by, and the ship continued to move in an erratic fashion, I came to the realisation that my mind had not been deceiving me; it was necessary that the captain immediately be informed. Now Captain Morehouse is a thoroughly good individual of excellent repute, but even I must admit I was fearful of telling him about my observations. But my apprehension was unfounded: the skipper listened attentively to my report of the mysterious ship, despite me having woken him from his sleep at such an unearthly hour.

Bewilderment grew as we observed the vessel: it was listing badly to starboard and then back again to port – drifting, spinning, and spiralling – as if in slow motion. Although I would never have suggested it to my captain for fear of ridicule, it seemed to me that the boat was being driven by the supernatural! When the captain finally lowered his telescope, I could see that he was immensely troubled and he at once advised me to rouse the crew in order that we might sail a little closer to the boat.

Whilst we remained one hundred spans away (so that our ship would come to no harm), we watched and waited for near on two hours, hoping that we might hear the crew or see a distress signal. Yet our keen ears could hear nothing apart from the cries of gulls overhead and the splash of waves against the ship's hull. Repeatedly, we tried in vain to attract the attention of the ship's crew until finally Captain Morehouse informed us that a small party would be boarding her, and I would be one of those to accompany him. Now, I am not a scared man, but I must admit that I wished he had not suggested such an idea!

Once aboard our rowing boat, we set off towards the ghostly galleon; every one of us felt a tremor of disquiet (even if we did not admit to it) and shivered despite the midday sun. After we had attached the rowing boat to the port stern of the ship, we climbed onto the deck, which was shrouded in silence. Descending below deck, we were greeted with many curious sights: the plates and glasses were laid out; there was plenty of food stored away; and the captain's cabin had a neatly-made bunk, where the sheets were turned back as if ready to be rested in.

As we ventured further into the ship, we turned to each other in bewilderment. Where were the crew? Had they been captured? If so, why was nothing disturbed or taken?

Year 6 model text 2: annotated

Dark grey highlights = Words from the National Curriculum word lists

The mystery of the Mary Celeste

12th December 1872
↑ date

What happened today was the strangest thing I have ever seen – or will
•••••••••••
dashes for parenthesis ↗
ever see – which is why I feel most obliged to record my faithful account
•••••••••••
↖ dashes for parenthesis
of the curious event. Perhaps, one day, someone shall read my hurried
↑ first person
notes about the mystery surrounding the Mary Celeste.
↑ expanded noun phrase

From my position in the crow's nest, where I had been keeping watch, my
↑ adverbial of place   ↑ relative clause   past tense ↗
eyes were drawn eastwards: dawn was fast approaching, which would
↖ past tense   ↖ colon
signal the end of my duty. Suddenly, emerging out of the early morning
     ↓ first person   adverbial of place ↗
mist, I could just about make out the vague outline of a ship. Now, this in
↖ adverbial of place   ↑ expanded noun phrase
itself is not unusual. Initially, my first thought was that it was a cargo ship
which was returning westwards: such ships carrying goods like wine and
↑ relative clause   colon ↗ ↑→ fact ————————————————→
clothes were familiar sights. However, upon closer inspection (and to my
↑→ fact ——————————————→ ↑ conjunctive adverb   brackets for parenthesis ↗
utter incredulity), I was made to realise that it was out of control.
•••••••••••
↖ brackets for parenthesis

↓ adverbial of time
As the seconds raced by, and the ship continued to move in an erratic
fashion, I came to the realisation that my mind had not been deceiving
     ↓ semi-colon
me; it was necessary that the captain immediately be informed. Now
    ↑→ subjunctive mood/form ————————→
Captain Morehouse is a thoroughly good individual of excellent repute,
                    ↑ expanded noun phrase
but even I must admit I was fearful of telling him about my observations.
                    ↑ opinion
But my apprehension was unfounded: the skipper listened attentively
                    ↑ past tense   ↖ colon
to my report of the mysterious ship, despite me having woken him
   ↑ expanded noun phrase
from his sleep at such an unearthly hour.

Bewilderment grew as we observed the vessel: it was listing badly
↑ **subordinating conjunction**   ↑ **colon**
to starboard and then back again to port – drifting, spinning, and
dashes for parenthesis ↗
spiralling – as if in slow motion. Although I would never have suggested
↖ **dashes for parenthesis**
it to my captain for fear of ridicule, it seemed to me that the boat was
being driven by the supernatural! When the captain finally lowered his
telescope, I could see that he was immensely troubled and he at once
advised me to rouse the crew in order that we might sail a little closer
to the boat.

Whilst we remained one hundred spans away (so that our ship would
↑ **subordinating conjunction**   **brackets for parenthesis** ↗
come to no harm), we watched and waited for near on two hours,
↖ **brackets for parenthesis**
hoping that we might hear the crew or see a distress signal. Yet our
first person ↗
keen ears could hear nothing apart from the cries of gulls overhead
and the splash of waves against the ship's hull. Repeatedly, we tried
↑ **expanded noun phrase**
in vain to attract the attention of the ship's crew until finally Captain
Morehouse informed us that a small party would be boarding her, and
I would be one of those to accompany him. Now, I am not a scared man,
↑ **conjunctive adverb**
but I must admit that I wished he had not suggested such an idea!

Once aboard our rowing boat, we set off towards the ghostly galleon;
↑ **adverbial of place**   ↑ **first person**   **semi-colon** ↑
every one of us felt a tremor of disquiet (even if we did not admit to it)
and shivered despite the midday sun. After we had attached the rowing
↑ **subordinating conjunction**
boat to the port stern of the ship, we climbed onto the deck, which was
relative clause ↗
shrouded in silence. Descending below deck, we were greeted with many
↖ **relative clause**
curious sights: the plates and glasses were laid out; there was plenty of
food stored away; and the captain's cabin had a neatly-made bunk,
hyphenated word ↑
where the sheets were turned back as if ready to be rested in.
↖ **relative clause**

As we ventured further into the ship, we turned to each other in
bewilderment. Where were the crew? Had they been captured?
rhetorical questions ↗
If so, why was nothing disturbed or taken?
↖ **rhetorical questions**

Recounts: newspaper articles

The purpose of a newspaper article is to inform and entertain the reader by providing news on current affairs.

Tips for teaching children to write newspaper articles

🐾 Engage children in the topic of newspapers and reporting by setting up a scene to 'investigate'. For example, an alien invasion or a break-in. You could ask adults in school to be eyewitnesses and allow the children to interview them. This can make it much easier for the children to write a report.

🐾 Invite children to consider other ways that news can be reported. Before writing a formal report, could the children create their own version of a news TV show such as Newsround? Record the children and play the recording back to them so that they can critique how informative their show was.

🐾 Choose an image or headline and ask children to write an orientation (the opening paragraph of a newspaper report) in groups. Remind them to use the five 'w's: who, what, where, when and why. You could make a table like the one below and make picture cards with options to go in each box to make this exercise even more accessible.

When	Who/what (subject)	Where	What happened?
On Monday night,	a missing airplane	from Iceland	was found.
Last week,	a protest	in Central London	was dispersed.

🐾 When children write newspaper reports, they can run the risk of writing a narrative that is too story-like. Remind children to avoid figurative or overly-descriptive language so that their reports remain factual.

🐾 Newspaper reports are a good chance to revise speech punctuation. You could use the acronym SCAPS to teach children how to correctly punctuate direct speech and the order in which punctuation marks should be used.

- **S: Speech marks**
- **C: Capital letter**
- **A: Actual words spoken**
- **P: Punctuation**
- **S: Speech marks**

🐾 Encourage children to use passive constructions in their writing. Teaching them how to use 'was' or 'were' with a past participle will help them to learn the construction.

- **was arrested**   • **was damaged**   • **was stolen**

🐾 Encourage more confident writers to consider bias. Can the children rewrite a news story with a different bias? For example, they could choose different language or write different witness statements.

'Working at greater depth' explained

🐾 There are two texts for Year 6 level in this chapter. The second Year 6 text on pages 156 – 159 is designed to show 'greater depth'.

- A formal tone and formal language are used throughout the news report.
- Exaggerated language is used to give a feeling of scandal and mystery: 'not only trespassed on their property but also dared to contact their precious daughter'.
- The author's bias comes across. In this case, the author has a negative view of Romeo, described as being mischievous.
- Eyewitness interviews provide longer quotations.
- Higher-level punctuation is used.
- More complicated vocabulary is used, such as 'divulged' (instead of 'said') or 'discontinue' (instead of 'stop').

Year 3 overview

Use this overview and the checklist alongside the Year 3 model text (pages 134 – 137).

🦖 Specific features for this text type

- A headline to attract the reader's interest — *Burglar Strikes Again!*
- A byline – the author of the article
- An orientation paragraph – a summary of the main points of the article — *Last night, multiple eyewitnesses spotted...*
- Body of the article – more detail about how the story unfolded
- Facts and statements — *The factory was broken into at 3:20 am.*
- Pictures and captions
- Quotations – extra detail and opinion — *"I just couldn't believe what I was witnessing," said Mrs Smith.*
- Reorientation – a final paragraph saying where the story might go next — *Police are still investigating...*
- Third person – formal language — *The eyewitnesses were present at the scene.*
- Past tense (mostly) — *arrested, damaged, caught, spotted, stole*

The following lists should be used as a tool to help teachers plan where to cover explicit grammar, punctuation and spelling objectives from both the Teacher Assessment Framework and the National Curriculum Programmes of Study.

🦖 Grammar

- Coordinating conjunctions – link ideas with 'but', 'so', 'and' or 'for' — *Road blockades were put in place so traffic could be redirected.*
- Subordinating conjunctions – expand upon independent clauses with 'when', 'so that', 'before' and 'until' — *DNA testing was carried out so that potential suspects can be identified.*
- Adverbs / adverbials of place — *the house above the shop*
- Adverbs / adverbials of time — *Last night, a jewellery shop was broken into...*
- Expanded noun phrases – add detail using 'from' and 'of' — *officers from the local police force*

🦶 Punctuation

- Apostrophes for possession   *the officer's response*

🦶 Spelling

- Year 3 / 4 words from the National Curriculum word lists: see page 9 of this book for a list of these. These words are highlighted in the Year 3 model text.
- Words ending in -tion, -sion, -ssion   *action, hesitation, expression, discussion, confession, permission, expansion, extension*

🦶 Checklist

Use this checklist with the Year 3 model text. See page 7 for more information.

Headline	
Byline	
Orientation	
Body	
Facts and statements	
Pictures and captions	
Quotations	
Reorientation	
Third person	
Past tense	
Grammar: Coordinating conjunctions	
Grammar: Subordinating conjunctions	
Grammar: Adverbs / adverbials of place	
Grammar: Adverbs / adverbials of time	
Grammar: Expanded noun phrases	
Punctuation: Apostrophes for possession	
Spelling: Year 3 / 4 word list	
Spelling: Words ending in -tion, -sion, -ssion	

Year 3 model text

THE LUNAR TIMES

MAN WALKS ON THE MOON!

21st July 1969
Lance Harris

Early yesterday morning (GMT time), American astronaut Neil Armstrong became the first man to ever walk on the Moon! People around the world tuned in for this world-famous event, which seemed like an impossible mission! It is sure to be an experience that this group of astronauts will remember forevermore!

The spacecraft, which is named Apollo 11, first went up into space on 16th July and carried three astronauts: Neil Armstrong, Buzz Aldrin and Michael Collins. Despite three astronauts being aboard the craft, only two landed on the Moon for Collins was to stay in orbit around the Moon in the mothership, Columbia.

↓ Neil Armstrong on the Moon

Whilst Collins orbited the Moon, Armstrong and Aldrin travelled via the lunar module – the Eagle – to land on the Moon's surface. It was so small that there was no room for seats, so the two astronauts had to stand up. As the intrepid explorers landed the lunar module, there was reportedly only thirty seconds of fuel left!

After waiting for twenty minutes before opening the hatch to the craft, at 02:56 am, Armstrong became the first human to step onto the Moon's surface, in an area known as The Sea of Tranquillity. This site had been selected because it looked smooth and safe for landing. This 'sea' is not, in fact, a sea but rather a lunar mare (dark markings on the Moon's surface formed by ancient volcanic eruptions). The brave astronaut then declared the words which are sure to become famous worldwide: "That's one small step for man, one giant leap for mankind."

On the Moon, the astronauts kept busy! The astronauts' jobs included taking photographs of their surroundings, collecting soil samples and performing various exercises so that the evidence could then be tested back on Earth.

One mission was to jump across the landscape! It is reported that Armstrong has commented, "The surface is like powdered charcoal and the landing craft has left a crater which is about a foot in depth!" The flag of the United States of America was planted at 03:41 am and a plaque bearing President Nixon's signature and an inscription was also unveiled.

These historic events were all captured on television cameras, which were installed on the spacecraft. The President was able to send a message to the two astronauts in which he described the pride of the American people. Although the astronauts were men, the trip would not have been possible without the brains of Katherine Johnson. Johnson carried out the calculations for the mission along with other women working at NASA.

This remarkable event marks the first time man has stepped foot on the Moon. It will be interesting to see how countries around the world will react and who the next man or woman on the Moon will be!

Year 3 model text: annotated

Dark grey highlights = Words from the National Curriculum word lists

THE LUNAR TIMES

MAN WALKS ON THE MOON!

↑ headline

21st July 1969

Lance Harris
↑ byline

↓ adverbial of time
Early yesterday morning (GMT time),
↓↑ orientation
American astronaut Neil Armstrong

became the first man to ever walk on the
↓ expanded noun phrase   adverbial of place ↗
Moon! People around the world tuned
↖ adverbial of place
in for this world-famous event, which

seemed like an impossible mission! It is
↑ word ending in -ssion
sure to be an experience that this group

of astronauts will remember forevermore!

↓↑ body
The spacecraft, which is named Apollo 11,
facts and statements ↗
first went up into space on 16th July
↖ facts and statements
and carried three astronauts: Neil
↖ facts and statements
Armstrong, Buzz Aldrin and Michael
↖↓ facts and statements
Collins. Despite three astronauts being

aboard the craft, only two landed on

the Moon for Collins was to stay in orbit
↑ coordinating conjunction
around the Moon in the mothership,

Columbia.

↓ **Neil Armstrong on the Moon**
↑ caption

↓↑ **body**
Whilst Collins orbited the Moon, Armstrong and Aldrin travelled via the lunar module – the Eagle – to land on the Moon's surface. *↑ apostrophe for possession* It was so small that there was no room for seats, so *coordinating conjunction ↑* the two astronauts had to stand up. As the intrepid explorers landed the lunar module, there was reportedly only thirty seconds of fuel left!

↓↑ **body**
After waiting for twenty minutes *↑→ adverbial of time* before opening the hatch to the craft, *↑ subordinating conjunction* at 02:56 am, Armstrong became the *↑ past tense* first human to step onto the Moon's surface, in an area known as The Sea of Tranquillity. This site had been selected because it looked smooth and safe for *facts and statements ↓→* landing. This 'sea' is not, in fact, a sea *↓→ facts and statements* but rather a lunar mare (dark markings *↓→ facts and statements* on the Moon's surface formed by ancient volcanic eruptions). The brave astronaut then declared the words which are sure to become famous worldwide: "That's *quotation ↗* one small step for man, one giant leap *↖ quotation   quotation ↗* for mankind." *↖ quotation*

↓↑ **body**
On the Moon, the astronauts kept busy! *↑ adverbial of place* The astronauts' jobs included taking *↑ apostrophe for possession* photographs of their surroundings, collecting soil samples and performing various exercises so that the evidence *subordinating conjunction ↑* could then be tested back on Earth.

↓↑ **body**
One mission was to jump across the *adverbial of place ↗* landscape! *↖ adverbial of place* It is reported that Armstrong has commented, "The surface is like *quotation ↗* powdered charcoal and the landing craft *↖ quotation   ↑ coordinating conjunction* has left a crater which is about a foot *↖ quotation* in depth!" *↖ quotation* The flag of the United States *expanded noun phrase ↗* of America was planted at 03:41 am *↖ expanded noun phrase* and a plaque bearing President Nixon's *apostrophe for possession ↗* signature and an inscription was also *↑ word ending in -tion* unveiled.

↓↑ **body**
These historic events were all captured *↑ third person* on television cameras, which were *↑ word ending in -sion* installed on the spacecraft. The President was able to send a message to the two astronauts in which he described the *expanded noun phrase ↗* pride of the American people. Although *↖ expanded noun phrase   subordinating conjunction ↑* the astronauts were men, the trip would not have been possible without the brains of Katherine Johnson. Johnson carried out the calculations for the *↑ word ending in -tion* mission along with other women working at NASA.

↓ **reorientation**
This remarkable event marks the first *↑ expanded noun phrase* time man has stepped foot on the Moon. It will be interesting to see how countries around the world will react and who the next man or woman on the Moon will be! *↑ adverbial of place*

Year 4 overview

Use this overview and the checklist alongside the Year 4 model text (pages 140 – 143).

🐾 Specific features for this text type

- A headline to attract the reader's interest — *Unidentified Flying Object!*
- A byline – the author of the article
- An orientation paragraph – a summary of the main points of the article — *In the early hours of this morning, residents of Benfleet witnessed mysterious lights in the sky...*
- Body of the article – more detail about how the story unfolded
- Facts and statements — *The object was spotted hovering 200 m above Benfleet Common.*
- Pictures and captions
- Quotations – extra detail and opinion — *"I couldn't believe my eyes," exclaimed Mrs Butler.*
- Reorientation – a final paragraph saying where the story might go next — *Specialist investigators are exploring the landing site...*
- Third person – formal language — *The discovery was made...*
- Past tense (mostly) — *landed, identified, investigated, experimented, photographed*

The following lists should be used as a tool to help teachers plan where to cover explicit grammar, punctuation and spelling objectives from both the Teacher Assessment Framework and the National Curriculum Programmes of Study.

🐾 Grammar

- Coordinating conjunctions – link ideas with 'but', 'so', 'and' or 'for' — *Investigators arrived quickly but were unable to capture any photographic evidence.*
- Subordinating conjunctions – expand upon independent clauses with 'when', 'so that', 'before' and 'until' — *Samples of the alien ectoplasm have been taken so that further information can be...*
- Adverbs / adverbials of time – say when events took place — *...landed as the sun was rising.*
- Adverbs / adverbials of place / preposition phrases – say where events took place — *Next to the river...*
- Expanded noun phrases – add detail using 'from' and 'of' — *samples from the landing site...*

🐾 Punctuation

- Apostrophes for possession   *one resident's reaction*
- Apostrophes with plural possession   *scientists' initial feedback...*

🐾 Spelling

- Year 3 / 4 words from the National Curriculum word lists: see page 9 of this book for a list of these. These words are highlighted in the Year 4 model text.
- Words ending in -tion, -sion, -ssion, -cian   *action, hesitation, expression, discussion, confession, permission, expansion, extension, politician*

🐾 Checklist

Use this checklist with the Year 4 model text. See page 7 for more information.

Headline	
Byline	
Orientation	
Body	
Facts and statements	
Pictures and captions	
Quotations	
Reorientation	
Third person	
Past tense	
Grammar: Coordinating conjunctions	
Grammar: Subordinating conjunctions	
Grammar: Adverbs / adverbials of time	
Grammar: Adverbs / adverbials of place	
Grammar: Expanded noun phrases	
Punctuation: Apostrophes for possession	
Punctuation: Apostrophes with plural words	
Spelling: Year 3 / 4 word list	
Spelling: Words ending in -tion, -sion, -ssion, -cian	

Peril in Pompeii!

25th August 79 AD
By Guido Alfonso

Last night, devastation hit the city of Pompeii. Mount Vesuvius erupted, surprising the residents who lived there, covering the city in millions of tonnes of volcanic ash and debris and killing approximately two thousand people.

It has been reported that there were a number of warning signs late yesterday afternoon, before the fatal eruption occurred. When a cloud of black smoke was noticed coming from the volcano, it was not known that the whole city would soon be lying in ruins for Vesuvius had laid dormant for almost one hundred years with no other recent eruptions. No one could have predicted the devastation that was about to happen. Soon after the cloud was spotted, a wave of rocks, gases and hot ash was hurled into the air and began to rain down over the north side of Pompeii.

Immediately, the city's alarm bells were sounded so that the residents could be evacuated but this was too little, too late for many! Although citizens were advised to evacuate, many refused to leave their homes and their personal belongings. Witnesses' statements describe how awful the event was.

A fortunate survivor of the eruption, Claudius, told the Vesuvius Chronicle: "As soon as I heard the bells, I grabbed my family and a few possessions and ran, but it was difficult to see where we were going or even to breathe because of the thick cloud of ash." He continued, "My relatives' injuries were small compared to that of other survivors, but I still have many nasty burns on my arms and legs. We had to use the river to soothe our scalded skin!"

Just after 8 pm, the volcano finally erupted sending boiling lava, molten rock and toxic gases into the air.

↑ **Blistering lava flowing from Mount Vesuvius**

This boiling lava then began to flow down the slopes towards the town, swallowing everything in its path and leaving a trail of destruction in its wake. The city was in ruins.

By early morning, It was believed that the eruption was finally over, but the tragedy is only just beginning, as the whole city of Pompeii has disappeared, lying beneath tonnes of volcanic dust and ash.

Has anyone survived? Will the city ever be lived in again? Perhaps, but it will be hard to tell until the ash has been cleared.

Many survivors have been observed trying to return to their homes to search for missing loved ones and lost valuables, but they have failed for the ash is still too hot. Many people couldn't search the city so groups of residents have abandoned all hope and fled to the nearby Bay of Naples in search of a new life. Those who remain will dig the city from its ruins, but it is unlikely that anything other than bones will remain.

Year 4 model text: annotated

Dark grey highlights = Words from the National Curriculum word lists

Peril in Pompeii!
↑ headline

25th August 79 AD

By Guido Alfonso
↑ byline

↓ orientation
Last night, devastation hit the city
↑ adverbial of time
of Pompeii. Mount Vesuvius erupted,

surprising the residents who lived

there, covering the city in millions
expanded noun phrase ↗
of tonnes of volcanic ash and debris
↖ expanded noun phrase
and killing approximately two
↑ coordinating conjunction
thousand people.

↓ body
It has been reported that there were a

number of warning signs late yesterday

afternoon, before the fatal eruption
subordinating conjunction ↑   word ending in -tion ↑
occurred. When a cloud of black smoke
↑ subordinating conjunction
was noticed coming from the volcano,

it was not known that the whole city

would soon be lying in ruins for Vesuvius
facts and statements ↑↓→
had laid dormant for almost one
↑↓→ facts and statements
hundred years with no other recent
↑↓→ facts and statements
eruptions. No one could have predicted

the devastation that was about to
↑ word ending in -tion
happen. Soon after the cloud was
adverbial of time ↗
spotted, a wave of rocks, gases and
↖ adverbial of time
hot ash was hurled into the air and

began to rain down over the north
adverbial of place ↗
side of Pompeii.
↖ adverbial of place

↓↑ body
Immediately, the city's alarm bells
↑ adverbial of time   ↑ apostrophe for possession
were sounded so that the residents
↑ subordinating conjunction
could be evacuated but this was too

little, too late for many! Although
subordinating conjunction ↑
citizens were advised to evacuate,

many refused to leave their homes

and their personal belongings.
↑ expanded noun phrase
Witnesses' statements describe
↑ apostrophe for possession (plural)
how awful the event was.

↓↑ body
A fortunate survivor of the eruption,

Claudius, told the Vesuvius Chronicle:
↓ quotation
"As soon as I heard the bells, I grabbed

my family and a few possessions and
word ending in -tion ↑
ran, but it was difficult to see where

we were going or even to breathe
↑ coordinating conjunction
because of the thick cloud of ash."
↓ quotation
He continued, "My relatives' injuries
apostrophe for possession ↑
were small compared to that of
coordinating conjunction ↓
other survivors, but I still have many
expanded noun phrase ↓↑
nasty burns on my arms and legs.

We had to use the river to soothe

our scalded skin!"

↓↑ body
Just after 8 pm, the volcano finally
↑ adverbial of time
erupted sending boiling lava, molten

rock and toxic gases into the air.

↑ **Blistering lava flowing from**
caption ↗

Mount Vesuvius
↖ caption

↓↑ body
This boiling lava then began to flow
past tense ↗
down the slopes towards the town,
↖ past tense
swallowing everything in its path and
↖ past tense
leaving a trail of destruction in its wake.
↖ past tense
The city was in ruins.
↖ past tense

↓↑ body
By early morning, it was believed that
↑ adverbial of time
the eruption was finally over, but the

tragedy is only just beginning, as the
expanded noun phrase ↗
whole city of Pompeii has disappeared,
↖ expanded noun phrase
lying beneath tonnes of volcanic dust
adverbial of place ↗
and ash.
↖ adverbial of place

↓↑ body
Has anyone survived? Will the city ever be

lived in again? Perhaps, but it will be hard

to tell until the ash has been cleared.
↑ subordinating conjunction

↓↑ reorientation
Many survivors have been observed

trying to return to their homes to

search for missing loved ones and

lost valuables, but they have failed

for the ash is still too hot. Many people
↑ coordinating conjunction
couldn't search the city so groups of
coordinating conjunction ↑
residents have abandoned all hope

and fled to the nearby Bay of Naples

in search of a new life. Those who
third person ↗
remain will dig the city from its ruins,
↖ third person
but it is unlikely that anything
↑ statement
other than bones will remain.

Year 5 overview

Use this overview and the checklist alongside the Year 5 model text (pages 146 – 149).

🐾 Specific features for this text type

• A headline to attract the reader's interest	*Naughty Nessy Hides Again!*
• A byline – the author of the article	
• Orientation – a summary of the main points of the article	*On Monday morning, a fervent photographer almost caught a glimpse of Scotland's most famous resident.*
• Body of the article – more detail about how the story unfolded	
• Facts and statements	*It was brought to worldwide attention in 1933.*
• Pictures and captions	
• Quotations – extra detail and opinion	*"I was so close to getting proof that this majestic beast exists!" exclaimed Walter McNally.*
• Reorientation – a final paragraph saying where the story might go next	*Walter has vowed to return to the loch in hopes of finally obtaining proof of this mysterious Scottish beast.*
• Third person – formal language	*A photograph was taken from the north side of the loch…*
• Past tense (mostly)	*taken, photographed, sighted, wondered, proved, exclaimed*

The following lists should be used as a tool to help teachers plan where to cover explicit grammar, punctuation and spelling objectives from both the Teacher Assessment Framework and the National Curriculum Programmes of Study.

🐾 Grammar

• Subordinating conjunctions – expand upon independent clauses with 'when', 'so that', 'before', 'until' or 'unless'	*Unless photographic evidence can be provided, the existence of the Loch Ness Monster will continue to be questioned.*
• Relative clauses – embed extra information	*The monster, which is believed to be twenty feet long, might reside in the…*
• Conjunctive adverbs	
○ Opposite points	*The investigation was stopped; however, Walter McNally has vowed to continue in his quest.*
○ Results	*Forensic zoologists are still investigating the evidence; as a result, the area surrounding the lake has been cordoned off.*

- Adverbs / adverbials of place   *from the depths of the loch*
- Adverbs / adverbials of time   *as twilight approached*

🐾 Punctuation

- Commas, brackets and dashes   *Loch Ness, which has a depth of 788 feet, has the largest*
  for parenthesis   *expanse of fresh water in Great Britain.*

🐾 Spelling

- Year 5 / 6 words from the National Curriculum word lists: see page 9 of this book for a list of these. These words are highlighted in the Year 5 model text.
- Words with hyphens   *world-famous, well-known, scale-covered*

🐾 Checklist

Use this checklist with the Year 5 model text. See page 7 for more information.

Headline	
Byline	
Orientation	
Body	
Facts and statements	
Pictures and captions	
Quotations	
Reorientation	
Third person	
Past tense	
Grammar: Subordinating conjunctions	
Grammar: Relative clauses	
Grammar: Conjunctive adverbs	
Grammar: Adverbs / adverbials of place	
Grammar: Adverbs / adverbials of time	
Punctuation: Commas, brackets and dashes for parenthesis	
Spelling: Year 5 / 6 word list	
Spelling: Words with hyphens	

THE GREEK GAZETTE

MARATHON MAN BRINGS NEWS OF VICTORY!

August 490 BC
By Darius Anagnos

Yesterday, a brave runner, whose name was Pheidippides, sadly died. The selfless hero was running to inform the Athenians of their miraculous victory against the Persian Empire and a possible second attack, before he tragically collapsed to the ground and died.

In recent weeks, the Athenian city-state has been under attack from the much larger Persian Empire. Sources suggest that King Darius – head of the Persian Empire – was keen to expand his empire so decided to invade Athens. With an army of approximately 25,000, the Persians were the likely victors; however, this was not to be the case.

Under the supervision of Commander Datis, the Persians sailed to Marathon, which is a few miles north-east of

Athens. Fully aware that they were severely outnumbered, the Athenians recognised the desperate need for cooperation and requested it from the most unlikely of allies: the Spartans. The Spartans are well-known for their fighting prowess so the Athenians sent a runner – Pheidippides – to ask for help. After running for two days and two nights, Pheidippides finally reached Sparta, which was over 130 miles away!

The Spartan army, who are usually strict enemies of the Athenians, immediately agreed to join forces with them when they heard that a foreign enemy was invading, but not until they had finished celebrating their festival. Pheidippides returned to Athens with the news that the Athenians would need to wait.

When interviewed, the leader of the Athenian army explained his decision to fight with the soldiers which were

↑ **Soldiers in battle**

available to him: "I knew we could not wait for the arrival of the Spartan army: it would be too late by then. Unless I thought of a plan quickly, my city would be attacked and I couldn't let that happen. I knew that Datis would place his strongest fighters in the middle so I placed my most experienced hoplites (soldiers) on the flanks so that we could attack the weaker fighters."

Despite sounding like a risky plan, this idea was a success! The Persian archers, who were positioned on the fringes of the attacking army, were easily charged down, leaving the Athenians free to close in and trap the remaining enemy soldiers. As a result, the general guaranteed victory for the Athenians, who only lost 192 men, compared to the death of over 6,000 Persians.

It was then that the hero of the hour (the runner Pheidippides) was sent to Athens from the battle site at Marathon, roughly 26 miles away, to share the news of the victory. However, when he arrived at the city, he was only able to shout a single sentence before falling to the ground and dying. A witness at the scene explained that he heard him shout the words "Nenikikamen!" which means "We have won!"

Pheidippides' determined effort has saved the Athenians from attack. Although it is essential that the city remains vigilant, leaders are hopeful that they will be able to stave off a future Persian invasion; thus, the current safety of Athens has been secured.

Year 5 model text: annotated

Dark grey highlights = Words from the National Curriculum word lists

THE GREEK GAZETTE

MARATHON MAN BRINGS NEWS OF VICTORY!

↑↓ headline

August 490 BC

By **Darius Anagnos**
↑ byline

↓ orientation
Yesterday, a brave runner, whose name
↑ adverb of time   commas for parenthesis ↗
was Pheidippides, sadly died. The selfless
↖ commas for parenthesis
hero was running to inform the Athenians

of their miraculous victory against the

Persian Empire and a possible second
↓ subordinating conjunction
attack, before he tragically collapsed to
                          past tense ↗
the ground and died.
↖ past tense

↓ body
In recent weeks, the Athenian city-state
↑ adverbial of time ↑   hyphenated word ↑
has been under attack from the much

larger Persian Empire. Sources suggest

that King Darius – head of the Persian
                    dashes for parenthesis ↗
Empire – was keen to expand his empire
↖ dashes for parenthesis
so decided to invade Athens. With an
                                fact ↗
army of approximately 25,000, the
↖ fact
Persians were the likely victors; however,
                        conjunctive adverb ↑
this was not to be the case.

↓↑ body
Under the supervision of Commander
↓↑ facts
Datis, the Persians sailed to Marathon,
↓↑ facts
which is a few miles north-east of
↑→ relative clause   ↑ hyphenated word

↓↑ body
Athens. Fully aware that they were

severely outnumbered, the Athenians

recognised the desperate need for

cooperation and requested it from the

most unlikely of allies: the Spartans. The

Spartans are well-known for their fighting
              ↑ hyphenated word
prowess so the Athenians sent a runner

– Pheidippides – to ask for help. After
↖ dashes for parenthesis   adverbial of time ↗
running for two days and two nights,
↖ adverbial of time
Pheidippides finally reached Sparta,

which was over 130 miles away!

↓↑ body
The Spartan army, who are usually strict
                          relative clause ↗
enemies of the Athenians, immediately
↖ relative clause
agreed to join forces with them when
                        subordinating conjunction ↑
they heard that a foreign enemy was

invading, but not until they had finished

celebrating their festival. Pheidippides

returned to Athens with the news that

the Athenians would need to wait.

↓↑ body
When interviewed, the leader of the

Athenian army explained his decision

to fight with the soldiers which were

Grammarsaurus KS2© Mitch Hudson and Anna Richards 2021

↑ **Soldiers in battle**
↑ caption

↓↑ body
↓→ quotation

available to him: "I knew we could not wait for the arrival of the Spartan army: it would be too late by then. Unless I thought of a plan quickly, my city would be attacked and I couldn't let that happen. I knew that Datis would place his strongest fighters in the middle so I placed my most experienced hoplites (soldiers) on the flanks so that we could attack the weaker fighters."

subordinating conjunction ↑

↑ adverbial of place

↓↑ body

Despite sounding like a risky plan, this idea was a success! The Persian archers, who were positioned on the fringes of the attacking army, were easily charged down, leaving the Athenians free to close in and trap the remaining enemy soldiers. As a result, the general guaranteed victory for the Athenians, who only lost 192 men, compared to the death of over 6,000 Persians.

relative clause ↗

↖ relative clause

↑ conjunctive adverbial

relative clause ↗

↖ relative clause

fact ↗

↖ fact

↑ **Soldiers in battle**
↑ caption

↓↑ body

It was then that the hero of the hour (the runner Pheidippides) was sent to Athens from the battle site at Marathon, roughly 26 miles away, to share the news of the victory. However, when he arrived at the city, he was only able to shout a single sentence before falling to the ground and dying. A witness at the scene explained that he heard him shout the words "Nenikikamen!" which means "We have won!"

↑ commas for parenthesis

conjunctive adverb ↗

↓ reorientation

Pheidippides' determined effort has saved the Athenians from attack. Although it is essential that the city remains vigilant, leaders are hopeful that they will be able to stave off a future Persian invasion; thus, the current safety of Athens has been secured.

third person ↗

↖ third person

↖ third person

↑ conjunctive adverb

Year 6 overview

Use this overview and the checklist alongside the Year 6 model texts on (pages 152 – 159).

🐾 Specific features for this text type

• A headline to attract the reader's interest	*HAUNTED!*
• A byline – the author of the article	
• Orientation – a summary of the main points of the article	*In the late hours of Sunday night, reports of screaming were heard...*
• Body of the article – more detail about how the story unfolded	
• Facts and statements	*The street is known for a host of paranormal activity.*
• Pictures and captions	
• Quotations	*"We don't know what happened," said the officer.*
• Reorientation – a final paragraph	*Detectives are on the scene to...*
• Third person – formal language	*Screaming was first heard...*
• Past tense (mostly)	*investigated, reported, questioned, arrived*

The following lists should be used as a tool to help teachers plan where to cover explicit grammar, punctuation and spelling objectives from both the Teacher Assessment Framework and the National Curriculum Programmes of Study.

🐾 Grammar

• Passive voice	*The suspects were located...*
• Subordinating conjunctions	*Before the event occurred, the family was asleep...*
• Relative clauses – embed extra information	*The street, which has had a host of paranormal activity recorded since the 1950s, is situated...*
• Conjunctive adverbs	
○ Additional points	*moreover, furthermore...*
○ Results	*consequently, overall...*
• Subjunctive mood/form	*The police recommend that all residents be cautious.*
• Adverbs / adverbials of place	*beneath the house*
• Adverbs / adverbials of time	*minutes after falling asleep*

🐾 Punctuation

● Semi-colons and colons	*He grabbed his weapon: he wanted to save his family.*
● Punctuation for parenthesis	*The family, who live in Hull, reported...*

🐾 Spelling

- Year 5 / 6 words from the National Curriculum word lists: see page 9 of this book for a list of these. These words are highlighted in the Year 6 model texts.

● Words with hyphens	*hi-tech, long-term effects, small-town event*
● Words ending in -able and -ible	*understandable, impossible*

🐾 Checklist

Use this checklist with the Year 6 model texts. See page 7 for more information.

Headline and byline	
Orientation	
Body	
Facts and statements	
Pictures and captions	
Quotations	
Reorientation	
Third person	
Past tense	
Grammar: Passive voice	
Grammar: Subordinating conjunctions	
Grammar: Relative clauses	
Grammar: Conjunctive adverbs	
Grammar: Subjunctive mood/form	
Grammar: Adverbs / adverbials of time / place	
Punctuation: Semi-colons / colons	
Punctuation: Commas, brackets and dashes for parenthesis	
Spelling: Year 5 / 6 word list	
Spelling: Words with hyphens	
Spelling: Words ending in -able and -ible	

THE LEADER POST

NORMANDY INVADED!

7th June 1944   **By Frank Chorley**

In the early hours of yesterday morning, an incredible operation, which combined the military might of more than twelve countries, took place on the beaches of Normandy, France. Operation Neptune – the code-name for the first stage of Operation Overlord – aimed to regain control from the devastating Nazi regime by combining the immense power of the Allies' naval, land and airborne forces. Winston Churchill – the British Prime Minister – asserted, "This vast operation is undoubtedly the most complicated and difficult that has ever taken place."

Just after midnight on 6th June, the operation began. It is believed that five key beaches were targeted so that the Allies had the best possible chance of gaining access into France. In the early hours of the morning, approximately 24,000 paratroopers were dropped

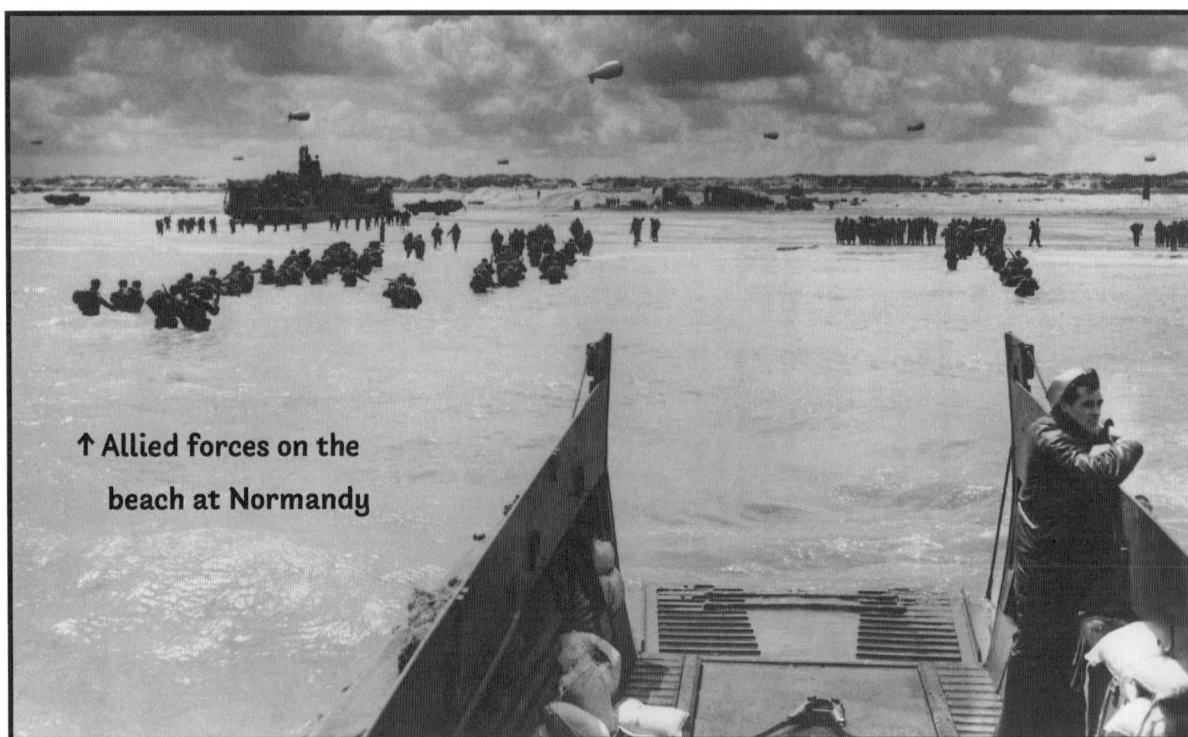

↑ **Allied forces on the beach at Normandy**

behind enemy lines, a few miles from the beaches, where the invasions would take place.

By 6:30 am, the beaches, where the water was shallow and ideal for a surprise attack, were occupied with soldiers wading towards the shores. These soldiers had arrived just hours earlier, travelling across the Channel that evening under the cover of darkness: they hoped their enemy would be taken by surprise.

As well as swimming and wading from the ships, some troops used amphibious vehicles (vehicles which can be driven on land or water) to gain access to the shore and begin the attack. Warships also fired at the German defences along the Atlantic Wall – an extensive system of fortifications built by the Nazis along the European coastline.

Furthermore, whilst the soldiers fought on the land, witnesses identified the Allied air forces taking to the skies throughout the day. Despite a strong attack from the Luftwaffe (the German air force), the Allied air forces were able to overpower the enemy. As a result, the Allied forces are now in a much more powerful position going forwards. Whilst it is

unknown how much impact the first day of fighting has had, it is hoped that this is a turning point in a war that has lasted far longer than anyone ever envisioned.

Reports returning to the UK remain infrequent and limited in information; however, according to the sources which are available, heavy casualties have been recorded during the Normandy Landings and, so far, the Allied troops have been unable to liberate all of the foreign beaches identified in Operation Neptune. It is also believed that the US troops on Utah beach came under heavy fire, with an estimated two hundred men either killed or injured. Sources positioned on Omaha beach have stated: "There have been over 2,400 US soldier casualties on this section of land alone."

Whilst the death of any individual – soldier or civilian – brings great sadness, it is hoped that their deaths will not have been in vain and this will be the beginning of the end of this devastating war. News will continue to be shared as soon as it becomes available. Meanwhile, the government advises that all those in the UK remain vigilant and pray for those fighting for our freedom.

Year 6 model text 1: annotated

Dark grey highlights = Words from the National Curriculum word lists

THE LEADER POST

NORMANDY INVADED!

↑ headline →

7th June 1944

By Frank Chorley
↑ byline

↓ orientation
In the early hours of yesterday morning,
↑→ adverbial of time
an incredible operation, which combined
↑ word ending in -ible   relative clause ↗
the military might of more than twelve
↖ relative clause
countries, took place on the beaches of
↖ relative clause
Normandy, France. Operation Neptune

– the code-name for the first stage of
↑ hyphenated word
Operation Overlord – aimed to regain

control from the devastating Nazi regime

by combining the immense power of the

Allies' naval, land and airborne forces.

Winston Churchill – the British Prime
                    dashes for parenthesis ↗

Minister – asserted, "This vast operation is
↖ dashes for parenthesis   quotation ↗
undoubtedly the most complicated and
↖ quotation
difficult that has ever taken place."
↖ quotation

Just after midnight on 6th June, the
↑ adverbial of time
operation began. It is believed that five
                              passive voice ↗
key beaches were targeted so that the
↖ passive voice   subordinating conjunction ↑
Allies had the best possible chance of
                    word ending in -ible ↑
gaining access into France. In the early
            adverbial of place ↑   adverbial of time ↗
hours of the morning, approximately
↖ adverbial of time   fact ↗
24,000 paratroopers were dropped
↖ fact

↑ **Allied forces on the**
   ↑ caption
   beach at Normandy

behind enemy lines, a few miles from
commas for parenthesis ↗
the beaches, where the invasions would
↖ commas for parenthesis
take place.

By 6:30 am, the beaches, where the
↑ adverbial of time   *relative clause ↗*
water was shallow and ideal for a surprise
↖ relative clause
attack, were occupied with soldiers
↖ relative clause
wading towards the shores. These soldiers

had arrived just hours earlier, travelling

across the Channel that evening under
↑ adverbial of place
the cover of darkness: they hoped their
colon ↗
enemy would be taken by surprise.

↓ fact
As well as swimming and wading from

the ships, some troops used amphibious

vehicles (vehicles which can be driven

on land or water) to gain access to the

shore and begin the attack. Warships

also fired at the German defences along

the Atlantic Wall – an extensive system
↑→ fact
of fortifications built by the Nazis along
↑→ fact
the European coastline.
↑→ fact

Furthermore, whilst the soldiers fought on
↑ conjunctive adverb   *past tense ↗*
the land, witnesses identified the Allied
↖ past tense
air forces taking to the skies throughout
adverbial of time ↗
the day. Despite a strong attack from
↖ adverbial of time
the Luftwaffe (the German air force), the

Allied air forces were able to overpower

the enemy. As a result, the Allied forces
↑ conjunctive adverb
are now in a much more powerful

position going forwards. Whilst it is

unknown how much impact the first day

of fighting has had, it is hoped that this
passive voice ↑
is a turning point in a war that has lasted

far longer than anyone ever envisioned.

Reports returning to the UK remain
third person ↗
infrequent and limited in information;
↖ third person   *semi-colon ↗*
however, according to the sources which

are available, heavy casualties have

been recorded during the Normandy

Landings and, so far, the Allied troops

have been unable to liberate all of the

foreign beaches identified in Operation

Neptune. It is also believed that the

US troops on Utah beach came under

heavy fire, with an estimated two

hundred men either killed or injured.

Sources positioned on Omaha beach
↑ adverbial of place
have stated: "There have been over
colon ↗   *quotation ↗*
2,400 US soldier casualties on this
↖ quotation
section of land alone."
↖ quotation

↓ reorientation
Whilst the death of any individual – soldier
dashes for parenthesis ↗
or civilian – brings great sadness, it is
↖ dashes for parenthesis   *passive voice ↗*
hoped that their deaths will not have
↖ passive voice
been in vain and this will be the beginning

of the end of this devastating war. News

will continue to be shared as soon as it
↓ word ending in -able
becomes available. Meanwhile,
subjunctive mood/form ↓
the government advises that all those

in the UK remain vigilant and pray

for those fighting for our freedom.

THE VERONA TIMES

HEIR TO THE MONTAGUES GATECRASHES BALL

By Louis Bolovio

2nd August 1346

Last night, when the Capulets were holding their annual masquerade ball, a worrying development occurred in the long-lasting feud between the Montagues and the Capulets. It has been reported that Romeo – the son of Lord Montague – was in attendance, despite knowing that his presence would reignite the violent hostility between these two prestigious Veronese families.

Sources at the ball have claimed that numerous sightings were made of the audacious young man, who was allegedly accompanied by two of his close friends. Some confusion still remains as those attending the party were all wearing masks; as a result, the identity of each guest could not be guaranteed. Whilst this ball is often viewed as the highlight of the social calendar, it is well-known that the invitation did not extend to the Montagues: the hosts' greatest rivals. Since the Prince of Verona's threat of death if the streets were yet again disturbed, an unlikely peace has ensued: neither family wishes to lose one of their own. However, this blatant act of rebellion is unlikely to go unnoticed by the proud Capulets.

Halfway through the evening, eyewitnesses claim that Romeo was seen standing to one side of the dance floor and was not participating in the dancing until he caught sight of Juliet, who is Lord and Lady Capulet's daughter. At this point, it has been suggested that he approached Juliet and attempted to take her hand: a move which could have resulted in disastrous consequences for the foolish boy for he was positioned in the very middle of the grand ballroom, surrounded by allies of the Capulets.

After speaking to the young girl for approximately twenty minutes, Romeo was seen sneaking out of the ballroom and into the night with his best friend Mercutio in tow, when he became aware that he was drawing unwanted attention to himself.

Many have questioned his motives. Was he really so arrogant to think he could get away with such an obvious flouting of the Prince of Verona's rules? According to some (more sympathetic) onlookers, who have requested to remain anonymous, he did not seem to have thought through his actions. When he was interviewed, one guest stated: "It was clear from his face that he wasn't in control of his body or his actions. It was quite romantic really! One minute he saw Juliet and then the next he was by her side!"

Clearly, this level of consideration is unlikely to be replicated by the hosts, who will no doubt be furious that the mischievous Romeo has not only trespassed on their property but also dared to contact their precious daughter.

Another of the reliable sources, Tybalt (Lord Capulet's nephew), has divulged that he recognised Romeo immediately

↑ **Decorated masks at the ball**

and planned to kill him on sight. However, Tybalt's uncle – Lord Capulet – forbade him from doing so: he did not want a scene to be created at a ball he was hosting. Moreover, he was only too aware of the warning given by the Prince of Verona; it is clear that a death on either side was something he was keen to avoid.

It remains to be seen whether this infatuation is genuine or an act to antagonise his enemy but understandably, the Capulets request that the citizens of Verona discontinue spreading rumours about the relationship between Romeo and Juliet. Authorities have made an appeal for anyone with further information on Romeo's motives to come forward at the next available opportunity.

Year 6 model text 2: annotated

Dark grey highlights = Words from the National Curriculum word lists

THE VERONA TIMES

HEIR TO THE MONTAGUES
↑↓ headline
GATECRASHES BALL

By Louis Bolovio
↑ byline

2nd August 1346

↓ orientation
Last night, when the Capulets were
↑ adverbial of time   relative clause ↗
holding their annual masquerade ball,
↖ relative clause
a worrying development occurred in

the long-lasting feud between the
↑ hyphenated word
Montagues and the Capulets. It has
                    passive voice ↗
been reported that Romeo – the son
↖ passive voice   dashes for parenthesis ↗
of Lord Montague – was in attendance,
↖ dashes for parenthesis
despite knowing that his presence

would reignite the violent hostility

between these two prestigious

Veronese families.

↓ body
Sources at the ball have claimed that

numerous sightings were made of
                    relative clause ↓→ ⟶
the audacious young man, who was
↓→ relative clause
allegedly accompanied by two of his
↓ relative clause →
close friends. Some confusion still remains

as those attending the party were all

wearing masks; as a result, the identity
       semi-colon ↗ ↑ conjunctive adverb
of each guest could not be guaranteed.

Whilst this ball is often viewed as the

↓↑ body
highlight of the social calendar, it is

well-known that the invitation did not
↑ hyphenated word
extend to the Montagues: the hosts'
                    colon ↗
greatest rivals. Since the Prince of

Verona's threat of death if the streets

were yet again disturbed, an unlikely

peace has ensued: neither family wishes
              conjunctive adverb ↓
to lose one of their own. However, this
                    passive voice ↗
blatant act of rebellion is unlikely to go
↖ passive voice
unnoticed by the proud Capulets.
↖ passive voice

↓↑ body
Halfway through the evening,
↑ adverbial of time
eyewitnesses claim that Romeo

was seen standing to one side of the
                    adverbial of place ↗
dance floor and was not participating
↖ adverbial of place
in the dancing until he caught sight of
              ↑ subordinating conjunction
Juliet, who is Lord and Lady Capulet's
       adverbial of time ↓   relative clause ↗
daughter. At this point, it has been
↖ relative clause
suggested that he approached Juliet
                    past tense ↗
and attempted to take her hand: a move
↖ past tense   colon ↗
which could have resulted in disastrous

consequences for the foolish boy for he

was positioned in the very middle of the
                    adverbial of place ↗
grand ballroom, surrounded by allies of
↖ adverbial of place
the Capulets.

↓↑ **body**

After speaking to the young girl for
adverbial of time ↗
approximately twenty minutes, Romeo
↖ adverbial of time
was seen sneaking out of the ballroom

and into the night with his best friend

Mercutio in tow, when he became aware
↑ subordinating conjunction
that he was drawing unwanted attention

to himself.

↓↑ **body**

Many have questioned his motives. Was
↑ third person
he really so arrogant to think he could

get away with such an obvious flouting of

the Prince of Verona's rules? According to

some (more sympathetic) onlookers, who
↑ brackets for parenthesis   *relative clause ↗*
have requested to remain anonymous, he
↖ relative clause
did not seem to have thought through his
↓ subordinating conjunction
actions. When he was interviewed, one
↑ passive voice
guest stated: "It was clear from his face
colon ↗   *quotation ↗*
that he wasn't in control of his body or his
↖ quotation
actions. It was quite romantic really!
↖ quotation
One minute he saw Juliet and then
↖ quotation
the next he was by her side!"
↖ quotation

↓↑ **body**

Clearly, this level of consideration is
passive voice ↗
unlikely to be replicated by the hosts,
↖ passive voice
who will no doubt be furious that

the mischievous Romeo has not only

trespassed on their property but also

dared to contact their precious daughter.

↓↑ **body**

Another of the reliable sources, Tybalt

(Lord Capulet's nephew), has divulged
↑ brackets for parenthesis
that he recognised Romeo immediately

↑ **Decorated masks at the ball**
↑ caption

↓↑ **body**

and planned to kill him on sight. However,
conjunctive adverb ↑
Tybalt's uncle – Lord Capulet – forbade
↑ dashes for parenthesis
him from doing so: he did not want

a scene to be created at a ball he was
adverbial of place ↑
hosting. Moreover, he was only too aware
↑ conjunctive adverb
of the warning given by the Prince of

Verona; it is clear that a death on either
↖ semi-colon
side was something he was keen to avoid.

↓↑ **reorientation**

It remains to be seen whether

this infatuation is genuine or an

act to antagonise his enemy but

understandably, the Capulets request
subjunctive mood/form ↗
that the citizens of Verona discontinue
↖ subjunctive mood/form
spreading rumours about the relationship

between Romeo and Juliet. Authorities

have made an appeal for anyone with

further information on Romeo's

motives to come forward at the

next available opportunity.

CHAPTER 6

Persuasive texts

The purpose of a persuasive text is to encourage the reader to buy a product or buy into an idea.

Tips for teaching children to write persuasive texts

🐾 Immerse children in the world of persuasive writing before they write their own persuasive texts! Encourage children to look at adverts in magazines or brochures and watch adverts on television so that they can identify how persuasive language is used.

🐾 Children could write persuasive texts in the form of a poster or even create their own radio or TV adverts. Ask the children to consider how they might need to change their text, depending on whether they're writing for TV or radio (where the listener won't be able to see the product).

🐾 If the children are writing a persuasive text about a real-life event, consider how their writing could be adapted to other non-fiction text types. The children could write a non-chronological report about the event or a diary entry from the perspective of someone who went to the event.

🐾 Encourage children to 'break the third wall' and write directly to a reader. Children can find it difficult to address a person they don't know. Finding a 'model' reader (imagining a specific person that they might write for) can help children to think about this. Sharing a picture of an imaginary reader can help too.

🐾 If children are writing about a product, invite the class to identify its unique selling point (USP). Write the USP on the board for children to see (make it the centre of a brainstorm). Annotate the USP with different language features children could use to explain the USP. For example, would they want to use an expert opinion to give the claims about the product credibility?

🐾 Encourage children to use a thesaurus and language clines to learn new persuasive vocabulary. A language cline is a scale of language that goes from one extreme to another, for example:

- **freezing**   - **cold**   - **cool**   - **warm**   - **hot**   - **boiling**

🐾 Create triples! Persuasive writing has so many examples of the rule of three. You could show children examples from speeches, adverts or film trailers.

🐾 Teach comparatives and superlatives when children are writing persuasive texts. Encourage the children to think about when it is appropriate to use comparatives and superlatives.

'Working at greater depth' explained

🐾 There are two texts for Year 6 level in this chapter. The second Year 6 text on pages 184 – 187 is designed to show 'greater depth'.

- The audience and purpose of the text is clear throughout the piece of writing.
- Exaggerated and exciting language has been used, such as the sentence, 'Never before has such an awe-inspiring variety of exhibits been housed in one location.'
- Ambitious vocabulary has been used throughout the text, such as 'sumptuous', 'opulent', 'prowess', 'spectacle' and 'extravaganza'.
- There are references to the historical period when this text was meant to have been written. For example, references to 'special ink to help blind people read' or the first public toilets.
- Despite the use of the personal pronoun 'you' throughout the text, the text is still relatively formal, through its use of language choices, syntax and punctuation.
- This is also supported by the use of the passive voice, for example, 'items are grouped'. By using an agentless passive, the sentence is more formal as it avoids determining who has grouped the items and makes the sentence more succinct.
- Higher-level punctuation is used.

Year 3 overview

Use this overview and the checklist alongside the Year 3 model text (pages 164 – 167).

🦖 Specific features for this text type

• Deals and bargains	*...and get 20% off.*
• Direct address to the reader (can include flattery)	*You deserve the best.*
• Alliteration and assonance	*the perfect price*
• Facts and statistics	*Nine out of ten dentists say that...*
• Opinion (can be expert opinion)	*Dr Paul agrees that...*
• Repetition	*a brighter smile for brighter days*
• Rhetorical questions	*Has tooth decay got you down?*
• Emotive / exaggerated language	*You'll have the whitest smile in just two days!*
• Triples / the rule of three	*whiter, brighter, happier smile*

The following lists should be used as a tool to help teachers plan where to cover explicit grammar, punctuation and spelling objectives from both the Teacher Assessment Framework and the National Curriculum Programmes of Study.

🦖 Grammar

• Adverbs – show possibility or degree	*You will definitely love...*
• Personal pronouns – speak directly to the reader with the second-person 'you'	*You deserve the best!*
• Expanded noun phrases – for exaggeration	*the brightest smile*
• Coordinating conjunctions – link ideas with 'and', 'for' or 'so'	*...and tell your friends!*
• Subordinating conjunctions – expand upon independent clauses with 'whenever', 'if', 'even if' or 'because'	*...because the formula is the best in the world!*
• Commands using the imperative – instruct the reader	*Buy today!*

🦖 Punctuation

- Commas for lists   *polish, brighten and whiten*
- Apostrophes for possession   *the toothpaste's formula*

🦖 Spelling

- Year 3 / 4 words from the National Curriculum word lists: see page 9 of this book for a list of these. These words are highlighted in the Year 3 model text.
- Words ending in -ous   *wondrous, marvellous, fabulous*

🦖 Checklist

Use this checklist with the Year 3 model text. See page 7 for more information.

Deals and bargains	
Direct address (can include flattery)	
Alliteration and assonance	
Facts and statistics	
Opinion (can be expert opinion)	
Repetition	
Rhetorical questions	
Emotive / exaggerated language	
Triples / the rule of three	
Grammar: Adverbs	
Grammar: Personal pronouns	
Grammar: Expanded noun phrases	
Grammar: Coordinating conjunctions	
Grammar: Subordinating conjunctions	
Grammar: Commands	
Punctuation: Commas for lists	
Punctuation: Apostrophes for possession	
Spelling: Year 3 / 4 word list	
Spelling: Words ending in -ous	

Marvellous Mike's travelling circus

Roll up! Roll up! The century's best circus has arrived in your town!

★ ★ ★ ★ ★

The largest, most spectacular show that you'll see this year is here! In fact, newspaper critics thought it was so impressive that they awarded it five stars which certainly shows we are worth visiting.

If you're looking for some family-filled fun, Marvellous Mike's circus is definitely the place for you! Are you still unsure? This highly popular show includes various acts such as heart-stopping performances from the world's best acrobats, death-defying stunt artists and side-achingly funny clowns! This circus includes sights that you will struggle to believe with your own eyes.

Because we want to be the best, Marvellous Mike promises to only show acts which have been pre-approved by audiences so there's no need to worry.

Book your tickets now if you want to avoid certain disappointment and ensure an experience of a lifetime. Even those people who claim to not enjoy circuses have had their opinions dramatically changed by our performers' incredible abilities! 99% of audience members said they will return to future shows even if they had previously disliked circuses! We're so sure you'll enjoy it that we'll refund your ticket's cost if you don't.

An extremely enjoyable, laugh-out-loud, entertaining extravaganza! It will be difficult to find a more exciting way to spend your time! What more is there to consider?

Buy your tickets before 1st February and you'll receive a free bag of popcorn to enjoy the show with. What more could you ask for?

Year 3 model text: annotated

Dark grey highlights = Words from the National Curriculum word lists

Marvellous Mike's travelling circus

↑ word ending in -ous

Roll up! Roll up! The century's best circus has arrived in your town!

↑ apostrophe for possession

★ ★ ★ ★ ★

direct address ↓

The largest, most spectacular show that you'll see

↑ expanded noun phrase

this year is here! In fact, newspaper critics thought

↑ expert opinion

it was so impressive that they awarded it five stars

↑ adverb for degree

which certainly shows we are worth visiting.

↑ adverb for possibility   ↑ personal pronoun

↓ subordinating conjunction
If you're looking for some family-filled fun, Marvellous Mike's

↑ personal pronoun   ↑ alliteration

circus is definitely the place for you! Are you still unsure?

This highly popular show includes various acts such as

↑ expanded noun phrase

heart-stopping performances from the world's best acrobats,

apostrophe for possession ↑   comma for list ↑

death-defying stunt artists and side-achingly funny clowns!

↑ alliteration

This circus includes sights that you will struggle to believe

with your own eyes.

Because we want to be the best, Marvellous Mike promises

↑ subordinating conjunction

to only show acts which have been pre-approved by

audiences so there's no need to worry.

↑ coordinating conjunction

Book your tickets now if you want to avoid certain disappointment

and ensure an experience of a lifetime. Even those people who
↑ coordinating conjunction

claim to not enjoy circuses have had their opinions dramatically
adverb for degree ↑

changed by our performers' incredible abilities! 99% of audience
statistics ↗

members said they will return to future shows even if they had
↖ statistics   subordinating conjunction ↑

previously disliked circuses! We're so sure you'll enjoy it that we'll

refund your ticket's cost if you don't.
↑ apostrophe for possession

↓ comma for list   exaggerated language ↗
An extremely enjoyable, laugh-out-loud, entertaining
↓↑ rule of three ──────

extravaganza! It will be difficult to find a more exciting way
↖ exaggerated language

to spend your time! What more is there to consider?
↑ rhetorical question ──────────→

Buy your tickets before 1st February
↑ command
and you'll receive a free bag of
↑ deal
popcorn to enjoy the show with.

What more could you ask for?
↑ repetition of 'What more' ──────→

POP
CORN

Year 4 overview

Use this overview and the checklist alongside the Year 4 model text (pages 170 – 171).

🦖 Specific features for this text type

• Deals and bargains	*Buy one get one free.*
• Direct address to the reader (can include flattery)	*You'll have the time of your life.*
• Alliteration and assonance	*an engaging experience*
• Facts and statistics	*95% of our customers*
• Opinion (can be expert opinion)	*Professor Plum has stated...*
• Repetition	*next generation gaming for the next generation of gamers*
• Rhetorical questions	*Are you ready to experience a gaming sensation?*
• Emotive / exaggerated language	*Experience the world through a new lens!*
• Triples / the rule of three	*next-generation graphics, unbelievable user experience and unparalleled technology*

The following lists should be used as a tool to help teachers plan where to cover explicit grammar, punctuation and spelling objectives from both the Teacher Assessment Framework and the National Curriculum Programmes of Study.

🦖 Grammar

• Adverbs – show possibility or degree	*Customers were so impressed that...*
• Personal pronouns – speak directly to the reader with the second-person 'you'	*This offer is just for you!*
• Expanded noun phrases – for exaggeration	*deal of the decade*
• Coordinating conjunctions – link ideas with 'and', 'for' or 'so'	*...so don't delay, buy today!*
• Subordinating conjunctions – expand upon independent clauses with 'whenever', 'if', 'even if' or 'because'	*If you're looking for a new gaming experience...*
• Commands using the imperative – instruct the reader	*Get your game in store now!*

🦕 Punctuation

- Commas for lists   *controllers, a gaming unit and VR goggles*
- Apostrophes for possession   *the console's technology*

🦕 Spelling

- Year 3 / 4 words from the National Curriculum word lists: see page 9 of this book for a list of these. These words are highlighted in the Year 4 model text.

🦕 Checklist

Use this checklist with the Year 4 model text. See page 7 for more information.

Deals and bargains	
Direct address (can include flattery)	
Alliteration and assonance	
Facts and statistics	
Opinion (can be expert opinion)	
Repetition	
Rhetorical questions	
Emotive / exaggerated language	
Triples / the rule of three	
Grammar: Adverbs	
Grammar: Personal pronouns	
Grammar: Expanded noun phrases	
Grammar: Coordinating conjunctions	
Grammar: Subordinating conjunctions	
Grammar: Commands	
Punctuation: Commas for lists	
Punctuation: Apostrophes for possession	
Spelling: Year 3 / 4 word list	

Year 4 model text

Ascend the astral throne!

Are you looking to find the love of your life?

Look no further because the manblob of the century, Astral King Vortigern, is single and looking for the perfect femblob – YOU!

Live in the lap of luxury!

Become the most popular femblob in the entire galaxy and live in style at King Vortigern's most famous astral home – Eden Palace. Inside this magnificent building, you will have personal guards at every door so you are not bothered by unwelcome guests.

Whenever you are feeling peckish, simply call upon the many servants you will have as the alien overlord and order the best food possible: sugared space beetles, orbital truffles and asteroid wine, just to name a few!

If you are lucky enough to marry this absolute hunk, then you'll also have exclusive discounts at all the shops in the galaxy.

What if you don't have any money?

Amazingly, King Vortigern is willing to marry even the poorest of femblobs.

"Don't worry about your gold, girls, because I've got plenty to share!"
– Our beloved Astral King Vortigern

All of Vortigerns's previous blobwives (and he has not really had that many!) absolutely loved their lives. Sadly, they have all died in non-suspicious, totally accidental ways. You can change this sorry situation, whilst becoming an instantly-rich queen of the blob people! The love of your life is not far away...

"King Vortigern is the most handsome manblob in all the land!" –
Threatened bystander

"He is so clever! His knowledge of the world is unbelievable. He is like a walking library!" –
Very important person

Year 4 model text: annotated

Dark grey highlights = Words from the National Curriculum word lists

Ascend the astral throne!

Are you looking to find the love of your life?
↑ personal pronoun 'you'   ↑ alliteration

Look no further because the manblob of the century, Astral King Vortigern, is single and looking for the perfect femblob – YOU!
direct address ↑

Live in the lap of luxury!
↑ alliteration
Become the most popular femblob in the entire galaxy and live in style at King
↑ expanded noun phrase
Vortigern's most famous astral home

– Eden Palace. Inside this magnificent
expanded noun phrase ↗
building, you will have personal guards
↖ expanded noun phrase
at every door so you are not bothered
↑ coordinating conjunction
by unwelcome guests.

Whenever you are feeling peckish,
↑ subordinating conjunction
simply call upon the many servants you will have as the alien overlord and order the best food possible: sugared space
↓ comma for list   rule of three ↗
beetles, orbital truffles and asteroid
↖ rule of three   rule of three ↗
wine, just to name a few!
↖ rule of three

If you are lucky enough to marry this absolute hunk, then you'll also have exclusive discounts at all the shops in
↑ deals
the galaxy.

What if you don't have any money?
↑ rhetorical question
Amazingly, King Vortigern is willing to
↑ adverb
marry even the poorest of femblobs.

"Don't worry about your gold, girls,
↑ command
because I've got plenty to share!"
↑ subordinating conjunction
– Our beloved Astral King Vortigern

All of Vortigerns's previous blobwives
↑ apostrophe for possession
(and he has not really had that many!)

absolutely loved their lives. Sadly, they
↑ adverb for degree
have all died in non-suspicious, totally accidental ways. You can change this sorry situation, whilst becoming an instantly-rich queen of the blob people!

The love of your life is not far away...
↑ repetition of 'love of your life'

↓ opinion
"King Vortigern is the most handsome manblob in all the land!" –
↓ **Threatened bystander**

"He is so clever! His knowledge of the world is unbelievable. He is like a
exaggeration ↗
walking library!" –
↖ exaggeration
Very important person

Year 5 overview

Use this overview and the checklist alongside the Year 5 model text (pages 174 – 177).

🐾 Specific features for this text type

• Deals and bargains	*Sign up and receive exclusive updates.*
• Direct address to the reader (can include flattery)	*You can really make a difference.*
• Alliteration and assonance	*sad stories*
• Facts and statistics	*Many animals need your help.*
• Opinion (can be expert opinion)	*The Royal Dog League has claimed...*
• Repetition	*Save a dog. Save a life.*
• Rhetorical questions	*Are you an animal lover?*
• Emotive / exaggerated language	*the heartbreaking cries of poor Rolo*
• Triples / the rule of three	*...feed, love and care for a puppy.*

The following lists should be used as a tool to help teachers plan where to cover explicit grammar, punctuation and spelling objectives from both the Teacher Assessment Framework and the National Curriculum Programmes of Study.

🐾 Grammar

• Modal verbs – for possibility	*Every animal should have...*
• Adverbs – show possibility or degree	*Feedback has been unbelievably positive.*
• Personal pronouns – speak directly to the reader	*You can make a difference.*
• Expanded noun phrases – for exaggeration	*the best life possible*
• Subordinating conjunctions – 'whenever', 'if', 'even if' or 'because'	*Even if you're strapped for cash...*
• Conjunctive adverbs	
◦ Additional points	*What's more...*
◦ Similar points	*Equally...*
◦ Opposite points	*In contrast...*
◦ Transition phrases	*As far as cost is concerned...*
◦ Results	*For this reason, we have...*
• Commands using the imperative – instruct the reader	*Adopt a dog today!*

🐾 Punctuation

- Commas for lists   *feed, love and save a puppy*
- Hyphens – for exaggerated descriptions   *a life-changing action*

🐾 Spelling

- Year 5 / 6 words from the National Curriculum word lists: see page 9 of this book for a list of these. These words are highlighted in the Year 5 model text.
- Words ending in -cial or -tial   *official, essential*
- Words ending in -able   *comfortable, reliable*

🐾 Checklist

Use this checklist with the Year 5 model text. See page 7 for more information.

Deals and bargains	
Direct address (can include flattery)	
Alliteration and assonance	
Facts and statistics	
Opinion (can be expert opinion)	
Repetition	
Rhetorical questions	
Emotive / exaggerated language	
Triples / the rule of three	
Grammar: Modal verbs	
Grammar: Adverbs for possibility / degree	
Grammar: Personal pronouns	
Grammar: Expanded noun phrases	
Grammar: Subordinating conjunctions	
Grammar: Conjunctive adverbs	
Grammar: Commands	
Punctuation: Commas for lists	
Punctuation: Hyphens	
Spelling: Year 5 / 6 word list	
Spelling: Words ending in -cial or -tial	
Spelling: Words ending in -able	

Year 5 model text

Join the Stellar Dome Community today!

A GLOBAL SPACE AGENCY-APPROVED FACILITY

Are you sick and tired of the constant aerial attacks from alien life forms on Earth? Wishing you could escape from crime, disease and pollution? Well, look no further than the stars, where you will find our brand-new Stellar Dome Community: the home away from home with no threat of alien invasion.

Guaranteed safety for all citizens!

Our state-of-the-art force field and laser defence system means you can sleep soundly at night knowing that you are protected from any destructive alien forces. Dr Spacegood of the Global Space Agency agrees that our protection system is stronger than anything planet Earth can offer.

No more tarmac means no more traffic!

You and your family deserve better than spending hours on end waiting in traffic. Instead, sit back and relax on our technologically-advanced colony monorail: a transport option fit for a king! Our ultra-fast, dependable trains travel around the base 24 hours a day, meaning you will always be on time!

100% PROTECTION FROM PLANETARY INVASION.

Grammarsaurus KS2© Mitch Hudson and Anna Richards 2021

"When I first talked to my husband about whether we should choose the astral swimming pool or the spacecraft landing pad for our home, we just couldn't decide. Luckily, the amazing staff at Stellar Homes organised a very reasonable price so we could afford both. So, even if you're strapped for cash, you can still get a bargain!"
Arabella Moon – resident

Comfortable living with artificial intelligence

Our marvellous space homes are stylish and spacious; what's more, each home has its own robotic staff to take away the troubles of cooking, cleaning and tidying, so you can get on with living. New residents were especially impressed by the range of options they could have built into their brand-new colony house.

Food, glorious food!

Whenever new citizens arrive at our space port to settle into their new homes, they cannot believe how good the food tastes. Not surprisingly, nine out of ten residents agree that our Stellar Dome Community foods taste better than the real thing back on Earth! That is because our special space farms grow the best-quality fruit and vegetables; even better, food prices are up to 30% lower at our orbital supermarkets compared to the prices on Earth.

Spectacular space leisure facilities and places of interest

No matter who you are and what you like, you will definitely find something extraordinary to do in our colony. If you're a thrill-seeker, then you will thoroughly enjoy plummeting deep into the dark canyons of neighbouring planet Alpha Teal 1. If you prefer to spend your time relaxing and shopping, then you will adore our HUD-50-N Mega Mall: four floors filled with all the clothes, furniture and entertainment you will ever need.

"It was the single most amazing experience of my life! The sights in the depths of those canyons will stay with me for life."
Rita Starr – resident

What are you waiting for? Join our space community today!

Year 5 model text: annotated

Dark grey highlights = Words from the National Curriculum word lists

Join the Stellar Dome Community today!

A GLOBAL SPACE AGENCY-APPROVED FACILITY

Are *you sick and tired of the constant aerial attacks from alien life forms on*
↑↓→ rhetorical question
Earth? Wishing you could escape from crime, disease and pollution? Well, look
↑ personal pronoun ↑ rule of three
no further than the stars, where you will find our brand-new Stellar Dome
↑ direct address ↑ hyphen
Community: the home away from home with no threat of alien invasion.

Guaranteed safety
for all citizens!

Our state-of-the-art force field and
↑ hyphens
laser defence system means you can

sleep soundly at night knowing that
↑ alliteration
you are protected from any destructive

alien forces. Dr Spacegood of the Global
expert opinion ↗
Space Agency agrees that our protection
↖ expert opinion
system is stronger than anything planet

Earth can offer.

No more tarmac means
no more traffic!

You and your family deserve better
↑ flattery
than spending hours on end waiting in

traffic. Instead, sit back and relax on

our technologically-advanced colony
expanded noun phrase ↗
monorail: a transport option fit for a
↖ expanded noun phrase
king! Our ultra-fast, dependable trains
hyphen ↑ ↑ word ending in -able
travel around the base 24 hours a day,

meaning you will always be on time!

100% PROTECTION FROM PLANETARY INVASION.
↑ statistics

"When I first talked to my husband about whether we should choose the astral
↑ modal verb
swimming pool or the spacecraft landing pad for our home, we just couldn't decide.
↑ modal verb
Luckily, the amazing staff at Stellar Homes organised a very reasonable price so we
↓ subordinating conjunction ↑ word ending in -able
could afford both. So, even if you're strapped for cash, you can still get a bargain!"
↑→ deals and bargains

Arabella Moon – resident

Comfortable living with artificial intelligence

Our marvellous space homes are stylish and spacious; what's more, each home
↑ conjunctive adverb
has its own robotic staff to take away the troubles of cooking, cleaning and tidying,
↑ comma for list
so you can get on with living. New residents were especially impressed by the range of options they could have built into their brand-new colony house.
↑ repetition of 'brand-new'

Food, glorious food!

Whenever new citizens arrive at our
↑ subordinating conjunction
space port to settle into their new homes, they cannot believe how good the food tastes. Not surprisingly, nine out of ten
statistics ↗
residents agree that our Stellar Dome
↖ statistics
Community foods taste better than the
exaggerated language ↗
real thing back on Earth! That is because
↖ exaggerated language

our special space farms grow the best-
↑ word ending in -cial   expanded noun phrase ↗
quality fruit and vegetables; even better,
↖ expanded noun phrase   conjunctive adverb ↑
food prices are up to 30% lower at our orbital supermarkets compared to the prices on Earth.

Spectacular space leisure facilities and places of interest

No matter who you are and what you like, you will definitely find something extraordinary to do in our colony. If you're
subordinating conjunction ↑
a thrill-seeker, then you will thoroughly
adverb for degree ↑
enjoy plummeting deep into the dark canyons of neighbouring planet Alpha Teal 1. If you prefer to spend your time relaxing and shopping, then you will adore our HUD-50-N Mega Mall: four floors filled with all the clothes, furniture
comma for list ↑
and entertainment you will ever need.

↓→ opinion
"It was the single most amazing experience of my life! The sights
in the depths of those canyons will stay with me for life."

Rita Starr – resident

↓→ rhetorical question
What are you waiting for? Join our space community today!
↑→ command

Year 6 overview

Use this overview and the checklist alongside the Year 6 model texts (pages 180 – 187).

🦖 Specific features for this text type

• Deals and bargains	*Get 10% off when you book three tickets.*
• Direct address to the reader (can include flattery)	*all you will ever need*
• Alliteration and assonance	*a mega mall*
• Facts and statistics	*100% guest satisfaction*
• Opinion (can be expert opinion)	*Dr Jude Byrne exclaimed that...*
• Repetition	*Act fast. Act now.*
• Rhetorical questions	*Are you ready for a family adventure?*
• Emotive / exaggerated language	*the best rides in the entire country*
• Triples / the rule of three	*thrill-seekers, animal-lovers and more*

The following lists should be used as a tool to help teachers plan where to cover explicit grammar, punctuation and spelling objectives from both the Teacher Assessment Framework and the National Curriculum Programmes of Study.

🦖 Grammar

• Modal verbs – for possibility	*You must try...*
• Active voice	*We have sold thousands of...*
• Adverbs – show possibility or degree	*You will definitely find...*
• Personal pronouns	*You and your family deserve better.*
• Expanded noun phrases – for exaggeration	*never-to-be-forgotten experience*
• Subordinating conjunctions	*Because we care about our clients...*

• Conjunctive adverbs
  – Additional points; similar points;
  opposite points; results; transition phrases
	*futhermore; similarly; in contrast;
	for this reason; as far as _____ is concerned*

• Commands using the imperative – instruct the reader	*Sign up now!*

🦖 Punctuation

• Semi-colons and colons	*Our prices are the lowest in Britain; you'll spend forever looking for a cheaper deal.*

- Hyphens   *thrill-seekers, animal-lovers and more*

🔥 Spelling

- Year 5 / 6 words from the National Curriculum word lists: see page 9 of this book for a list of these. These words are highlighted in the Year 6 model texts.
- Words ending in -cial or -tial   *artificial, essential*
- Words ending in -able   *reasonable, dependable*

🔥 Checklist

Use this checklist with the Year 6 model texts. See page 7 for more information.

Deals and bargains	
Direct address (can include flattery)	
Alliteration and assonance	
Facts and statistics	
Repetition	
Rhetorical questions	
Emotive / exaggerated language	
Triples / the rule of three	
Grammar: Modal verbs	
Grammar: Active voice	
Grammar: Adverbs for possibility / degree	
Grammar: Personal pronouns	
Grammar: Expanded noun phrases	
Grammar: Subordinating conjunctions	
Grammar: Conjunctive adverbs	
Grammar: Commands	
Punctuation: Semi-colons and colons	
Punctuation: Hyphens	
Spelling: Year 5 / 6 word list	
Spelling: Words ending in -cial or -tial	
Spelling: Words ending in -able	

Join the Women's Land Army

**Do the right thing and make your country proud:
become one of Britain's Land Girls today!**

Are you reliable, hard-working and patriotic? Then this could be the perfect profession for you! For a healthy, happy job, you should definitely choose the Women's Land Army. What have you got to lose?

Food comes first

It is now necessary for us to grow more food at home. This is especially true in the weeks and months ahead because German forces are destroying cargo ships in the oceans surrounding our great land, which is preventing our previously imported food from reaching us. We must use our land to provide essential food for our troops and civilians. Our brave, self-sacrificing men are at war

for your freedom; for this reason, you need to become the country's new, rural workforce. It's time for you to do your bit and support the war effort. Do you think you have the skills to support the government in this important initiative?

Do your duty

If you are a woman aged between 19 and 43, then this marvellous opportunity will enable you to serve your country with pride and join the thousands of other women who have already selflessly signed up. Worried that you don't have the physical strength to support your country in this way? Fear not! Even if you don't have any previous experience in this area, we assure you that there is a role for you: any help is appreciated in our attempts to defeat our common enemy.

No job too small

Are you concerned that you don't have the skills required to work on the land? The Women's Land Army has a variety of roles which need to be filled: milking cows, lambing, managing poultry,

Grammarsaurus KS2© Mitch Hudson and Anna Richards 2021

gathering crops, digging ditches, catching rats and carrying out farm maintenance work. What's more, larger tasks such as driving heavy machinery – excavators and tractors – are also important, as we attempt to reclaim land for food production. There is a job for every individual who applies; don't let the fear of failure and inexperience stop you from making the right decision!

Endless opportunities

Do you wish to learn exciting and interesting new skills whilst meeting people from a range of backgrounds? Joining the Women's Land Army promises to provide you with never-to-be-forgotten experiences as well as a healthier, outdoor lifestyle and the chance to make lifelong friends. If you live in a dirty, polluted town or city, this opportunity could significantly improve your health as well as support our soldiers. What's stopping you? For those dedicated recruits who are leaving their home towns, there are currently seven hundred, comfortable hostels ready to accommodate you. As far as pay is concerned, you'll be rewarded for your patriotism with an excellent wage. Earn 28 shillings a week, with 14 shillings deducted for food and accommodation: we recognise your hard work and our wages reflect this appreciation!

It is essential that we keep the farms going while our soldiers are fighting for our freedom!

Year 6 model text 1: annotated

Dark grey highlights = Words from the National Curriculum word lists

Join the Women's Land Army

Do the right thing and make your country proud:
colon ↗
become one of Britain's Land Girls today!

Are you reliable, hard-working and
word ending in -able ↑   ↑ hyphen
patriotic? Then this could be the perfect
modal verb ↑
profession for you! For a healthy, happy
↑ alliteration
job, you should definitely choose the
Women's Land Army. What have you
↑ rhetorical question
got to lose?

for your freedom; for this reason, you
semi-colon ↓   ↓ conjunctive adverb   personal pronoun ↓
need to become the country's new, rural
expanded noun phrase ↓
↓ expanded noun phrase
workforce. It's time for you to do your
↑ → direct address
bit and support the war effort. Do you
↑ → direct address
think you have the skills to support the
government in this important initiative?

Food comes first

↓ → active voice
It is now necessary for us to grow more
↓ → active voice
food at home. This is especially true in
adverb for degree ↑
the weeks and months ahead because
subordinating conjunction ↑
German forces are destroying cargo
ships in the oceans surrounding our great
land, which is preventing our previously
imported food from reaching us. We
must use our land to provide essential
↑ modal verb   word ending in -tial ↑
food for our troops and civilians. Our
brave, self-sacrificing men are at war
↖ hyphen

Do your duty

If you are a woman aged between 19
and 43, then this marvellous opportunity
will enable you to serve your country
↑ modal verb   repetition of 'your country' ↑
with pride and join the thousands of
other women who have already selflessly
alliteration ↗
signed up. Worried that you don't have
↖ alliteration
the physical strength to support your
↓ command
country in this way? Fear not! Even if you
subordinating conjunction ↑
don't have any previous experience in
this area, we assure you that there is a
role for you: any help is appreciated in our
↑ colon
attempts to defeat our common enemy.

No job too small

Are you concerned that you don't have
↑ personal pronoun
the skills required to work on the land?
↓ facts
The Women's Land Army has a variety
of roles which need to be filled: milking
colon ↗
cows, lambing, managing poultry,

gathering crops, digging ditches,
comma for list ↗
catching rats and carrying out farm

maintenance work. What's more, larger

tasks such as driving heavy machinery

– excavators and tractors – are also

important, as we attempt to reclaim land

for food production. There is a job for

every **individual** who applies; don't let the
semi-colon ↗
fear of failure and inexperience stop you

from making the right decision!

Endless opportunities

Do you wish to learn exciting and
↑ rhetorical question
interesting new skills whilst meeting

people from a range of backgrounds?
↓ facts
Joining the Women's Land Army

promises to provide you with never-
hyphens ↗
to-be-forgotten experiences as well
↖ hyphens
as a healthier, outdoor lifestyle and

↑↓ facts
the chance to make lifelong friends.
expanded noun phrase ↓
If you live in a dirty, polluted town or
↓ expanded noun phrase
city, this opportunity could significantly
modal verb ↗   adverb for degree ↑
improve your health as well as **support**
alliteration ↗
our soldiers. What's stopping you? For
↖ alliteration
those dedicated recruits who are leaving
↓→ facts
their home towns, **there** are currently

seven hundred, comfortable hostels
↑ word ending in -able
ready to **accommodate** you. As far as
conjunctive adverb ↗
pay is concerned, you'll be rewarded for

your patriotism with an **excellent** wage.
↓ facts
Earn 28 shillings a week, with 14 shillings

deducted for food and accommodation:
colon ↗
we **recognise** your hard work and our

wages reflect this appreciation!

It is essential that we keep the

farms going while our soldiers

are fighting for our freedom!
↑ emotive language

Visit the Great Exhibition

1st May – 15th October 1851

The Great Exhibition: a triumph in engineering; a spectacle of industry and progress; Prince Albert's magnificent masterpiece. It's here, on your doorstep. To miss the opportunity to visit this presentation of wonder and innovation would be very foolish indeed: this is the world's first display of design and manufacturing! Never before has such an awe-inspiring variety of exhibits been housed in one location. What are you waiting for?

At 1,850 feet long and 108 feet high – high enough to accommodate two great elm trees – this palace, which is situated in Hyde Park, houses the wonders of the world just for you!

This incredibly impressive structure – the country's very own 'crystal palace' – is essential viewing and should not be missed by you, your family or your friends. Tell everyone you know to attend this marvellous display of manufacturing prowess. We guarantee enjoyment for all! The Great Exhibition includes every marvel of the Victorian Age!

If you want your curiosity to be awakened, then a visit to the exhibition is a must. The exhibition features a myriad of items from the international stage; indeed, a staggering 100,000 objects provided by over 14,000 exhibits are estimated to be displayed in this one location. For your ease, the items are grouped into four principle themes: machinery, manufactures, fine arts and raw materials. From the British Empire and beyond, visit this palace of wonders to see objects you never before thought imaginable: state-of-the-art vehicles, sumptuous tapestries, exotic silk clothes and opulent perfumes. Even fully-constructed houses have been erected!

Regardless of your background, there will definitely be something here to arouse your interest, no matter how bizarre or unique! That is our promise to you. Do you need further persuasion? As Queen Victoria – our majestic leader and most dependable and frequent guest – has stated, every conceivable invention can be found here! Whenever you need inspiration, visit us, for here you will find a whole host of magnificent marvels. Objects of note include special ink to help blind people read, folding pianos and extremely valuable and rare gems and jewels – including a gem with inestimable value, the Koh-i-Noor diamond.

Join the six million people who have already made the sensible decision to visit the pride of the British Empire. If it's good enough for a third of the British population, surely it's good enough for you? Regardless of where you live in the country, a visit to this excellent extravaganza should be planned immediately. Britain's rapidly expanding railway network will provide the required transport links; for this reason, failure to attend is inexcusable. Special excursion trips via rail can be booked with prices as low as five shillings. What's more, for the first time ever, 'waiting rooms and conveniences' are provided, where, for the cost of one penny, you shall have the blessing of a private cubicle.

Prices

Undoubtedly, this is an experience which cannot be missed; therefore, the price of admission has been reduced (from £3 for gentlemen and £2 for ladies) to only a shilling per person so that everyone is able to appreciate this extraordinary fair!

Year 6 model text 2: annotated

Dark grey highlights = Words from the National Curriculum word lists

Visit the Great Exhibition

1st May – 15th October 1851

colon ↓ ↓→ rule of three

The Great Exhibition: a triumph in engineering; a spectacle of industry

↓→ rule of three

and progress; Prince Albert's magnificent masterpiece. It's here, on your

↑ alliteration — direct address ↗

doorstep. To miss the opportunity to visit this presentation of wonder and

↖ direct address

innovation would be very foolish indeed: this is the world's first display of

↑ modal verb — ↖ colon

design and manufacturing! Never before has such an awe-inspiring variety

hyphen ↑

of exhibits been housed in one location. What are you waiting for?

rhetorical question ↑

At 1,850 feet long and 108

fact ↗

feet high – high enough to

↖ fact

accommodate two great elm trees –

this palace, which is situated in Hyde

Park, houses the wonders of the world

↑ alliteration

just for you!

↑ personal pronoun

This incredibly impressive

↑ exaggerated language

structure – the country's very own

'crystal palace' – is essential viewing

word ending in -tial ↗

and should not be missed by you, your

triple ↗

family or your friends. Tell everyone

↖ triple — active voice ↗

you know to attend this marvellous

↖ active voice

display of manufacturing prowess.

We guarantee enjoyment for all! The

↑ personal pronoun

Great Exhibition includes every marvel

of the Victorian Age!

If you want your curiosity to

↑ subordinating conjunction

be awakened, then a visit to the

exhibition is a must. The exhibition

features a myriad of items from the

semi-colon ↓ expanded noun phrase ↗

international stage; indeed, a staggering

↖ expanded noun phrase — ↑ conjunctive adverb

100,000 objects provided by over 14,000

exhibits are estimated to be displayed in

this one location. For your ease, the items

are grouped into four principle themes:

colon ↗

machinery, manufactures, fine arts and

raw materials. From the British Empire

and beyond, visit this palace of wonders

↑ active voice

to see objects you never before thought

↓ hyphens

imaginable: state-of-the-art vehicles,

↑ word ending in -able

sumptuous tapestries, exotic silk clothes

and opulent perfumes. Even fully-

hyphen ↗

constructed houses have been erected!

↖ hyphen

Regardless of your background,
↑ personal pronoun
there will definitely be something
modal verb ↑ ↑ adverb for possibility
here to arouse your interest, no matter

how bizarre or unique! That is our promise
↓ rhetorical question   deal ↗
to you. Do you need further persuasion? As
↖ deal
Queen Victoria – our majestic leader and

most dependable and frequent guest
    ↑ word ending in -able
– has stated, every conceivable invention

can be found here! Whenever you need
                    ↑ subordinating conjunction
inspiration, visit us, for here you will find a

whole host of magnificent marvels.

Objects of note include special ink to help

blind people read, folding pianos and
              ↑ comma for list
extremely valuable and rare gems and

jewels – including a gem with inestimable
                        word ending in -able ↑
value, the Koh-i-Noor diamond.

Join the six million people who
↑ command
have already made the sensible

decision to visit the pride of the British
        ↓ repetition of 'good' ⟶
Empire. If it's good enough for a third of
↓↑ repetition of 'good' ⟶
the British population, surely it's good
↓↑ repetition of 'good'   ↑ adverb for possibility
enough for you? Regardless of where you

live in the country, a visit to this excellent
                                    exaggeration ↗
extravaganza should be planned
↖ exaggeration   ↑ modal verb
immediately. Britain's rapidly expanding
                        expanded noun phrase ↗
railway network will provide the required
↖ expanded noun phrase
transport links; for this reason, failure to
        semi-colon ↑   ↑ conjunctive adverb
attend is inexcusable. Special excursion
        word ending in -able ↑ ↑ word ending in -cial
trips via rail can be booked with prices as

low as five shillings. What's more, for the
                            ↑ conjunctive adverb
first time ever, 'waiting rooms and

conveniences' are provided, where, for
                        modal verb ↓
the cost of one penny, you shall have the
                        expanded noun phrase ↗
blessing of a private cubicle.
↖ expanded noun phrase

Prices
        ↓ adverb for degree
Undoubtedly, this is an
            emotive language ↗
experience which cannot be
↖ emotive language
missed; therefore, the price of
↖ emotive language   bargain ↗
admission has been reduced
↖ bargain
(from £3 for gentlemen and

£2 for ladies) to only a shilling

per person so that everyone

is able to appreciate this
            expanded noun phrase ↗
extraordinary fair!
↖ expanded noun phrase

Glossary of terms

Term	Meaning	Example
active voice	When a sentence is in the active voice, the subject is doing the action.	*Holly opened the door.*
adjective	A word that describes a noun.	*tiny, big, generous*
adverb	A word that describes and qualifies a verb, adjective or another adverb.	*quickly, soon*
adverbial	A group of words that is used to indicate time, place, manner or frequency.	*After school, I attended football club.*
antonym	A word opposite in meaning to another word.	*bad / good* *beautiful / ugly*
apostrophe	For omission: to replace letters which have been omitted. For possession: to show something belongs to someone or something.	*should not / shouldn't* *Jithu's jumper*
brackets	A pair of marks used for parenthesis.	*Queen Elizabeth II (Britain's longest-reigning monarch) was crowned in 1953.*
bullet points	Used for lists.	• *sugar* • *butter* • *flour*
capital letter	Used at the start of a sentence or for a proper noun.	*My cousin lives in Scotland.*
clause	A part of a sentence that contains a subject and a verb.	*I went to my friend's house.*
cohesion	Using words and phrases to link paragraphs or sentences to help guide a reader.	*It was beginning to rain. However, the children could still go outside as they had umbrellas.*

Grammarsaurus KS2© Mitch Hudson and Anna Richards 2021

Term	Meaning	Example
colon	Used to detail the previous clause by answering or explaining the idea within it. Colons can be used at the start of a list if there is an independent clause before the punctuation.	*The verdict had been reached: guilty!* *I packed only essential items in my bag: a toothbrush, a hairbrush and some pyjamas.*
comma	Used to separate items in a list and for a parenthesis.	*I packed my teddy bear, pyjamas and a toothbrush.* *The Eiffel Tower, which is located in Paris, is 324 m high.*
command	A sentence (beginning with an imperative verb) which tells someone to do something. It can end with an exclamation mark or a full stop.	*Put your toys away.* *Stop what you're doing!*
coordinating conjunction	A word used to join independent clauses in a sentence.	*for, and, nor, but, or, yet, so*
dashes	These marks can be used like brackets or to introduce a new clause.	*I put your present in the post – it will arrive in three days.*
determiner	A word that introduces a noun and can give more detail.	*a, the, some, any, my, your*
direct speech	Writing the actual words of a speaker using inverted commas (speech marks).	*"Where are you?" Jason asked.*
ellipsis	Used to show that one or more words have been missed out or that a sentence is not finished.	*But who knew what horrors lurked behind the door…*
exclamation	A group of words or sentence which shows surprise, emotion or pain. It does not have to include 'what' or 'how' unless you want it to be an exclamation sentence (see below).	*I did it!*
exclamation mark	A mark at the end of an exclamation or exclamation sentence.	*It was raining again!*
exclamation sentence	A sentence which shows surprise, emotion or pain. It ends with an exclamation mark and must start with either 'what' or 'how' and include a verb.	*What a wonderful day it is!*
expanded noun phrase	A group of words that serves the same function as a noun in a clause.	*a scary giant* *a witch on a broom*

Term	Meaning	Example
hyphen	Used to connect two or more words.	*dagger-like, twenty-one*
inverted commas	Used at the start and end of direct speech (and are also known as speech marks).	*"Let's go!" said mum.*
modal verb	Used to express ideas such as possibility, intention, obligation and necessity.	*can, could, should, might, shall, ought to*
noun	A person, place or thing.	*Queen Elizabeth, London, crown*
parenthesis	A word or phrase inserted as an explanation or afterthought (can be punctuated with brackets, dashes or commas).	*Julia – my auntie – gave me a brilliant birthday present.*
passive voice	When a sentence is in the passive voice, the subject of the sentence is acted on by the verb.	*The door was opened by Aisha.*
past / present / future tense	Past: something happened / has happened. Present: something happens / is happening. Future: something will happen / is going to happen.	*I was* *I am* *I will be / I'm going to be*
plural	More than one thing.	*two men* *two dogs* *two babies*
possessive pronoun	A pronoun showing possession.	*mine, yours, his, hers, ours, theirs*
prefix	Letters added to the start of a word.	*disagree, unhappy*
preposition	A word which shows a noun's relationship to another word in the sentence. It often shows where or when something is.	*under, over, before, beside*
pronoun	A word used to replace a noun.	*I, she, they, his, them*
punctuation	Marks we use in writing.	*. / , / ? / !*
question	Something you ask. It ends with a question mark.	*What is your name?*
question mark	A mark to show the end of a question.	*How will the story end?*
relative clause	Used to explain or describe something that has just been mentioned.	*The dog, which was black and white, chased after the ball.*
relative pronoun	A pronoun that introduces a relative clause.	*when, who, which, where, that, whom*

Grammarsaurus KS2© Mitch Hudson and Anna Richards 2021

Term	Meaning	Example
semi-colon	A punctuation mark used to separate longer, detailed items in a list or to link related clauses.	*She noticed three things: there was dirt on the wall; the door was broken, hanging off one hinge; and the smell was disgusting.* *It was starting to snow; the children grabbed their scarves and gloves.*
sentence	A group of words with a verb that makes complete sense.	*The man had a dog.*
singular	One thing.	*one man* *one dog* *one baby*
statement	A sentence which states something. It ends with a full stop.	*I like animals.* *I feel happy.*
subjunctive mood/form	Used to express doubt, wishes or a recommendation.	*The police have recommended that all drivers stay clear of the city centre.*
subordinate clause	A clause that doesn't make sense on its own. It begins with a subordinating conjunction.	*I ate my dinner quickly because I was hungry.*
subordinating conjunction	A word at the start of a subordinate clause.	*because, when, if, unless*
suffix	Letters added to the end of a root word.	*jumping, beautiful*
synonym	A word that means exactly or nearly the same as another word.	*smile / grin* *black / ebony*
verb	An action.	*run, walk, jump*

Further teaching tips and acronyms

Over the years, we have used a range of acronyms and teaching ideas which have helped us when teaching non-fiction writing. Check out some of our favourites below.

🐾 Coordinating conjunctions: FANBOYS

You can use the acronym FANBOYS to teach the different coordinating conjunctions.

I am going shopping and I am buying food for dinner.

F	for
A	and
N	nor
B	but
O	or
Y	yet
S	so

🐾 Formal / informal

This table will help children identify when they might use a formal or informal tone of voice. Remember that sometimes children might need to use formal and informal language, for example, in an advert they might change from a formal to an informal tone to address the reader directly.

Formal	Informal
A letter to a gas company	A message to a friend
A job application	An email to your cousin
A police report	A postcard
A letter of complaint	A note to your parents

Formal	Informal
Avoid contractions *will not*	Use contractions *won't*
Avoid slang / colloquial language *It is raining heavily.*	Use slang / colloquial language *It's raining cats and dogs.*
Use formal equivalence *Stop eavesdropping.*	Use phrasal verbs *Stop listening in.*
Avoid question tags *That is right.*	Use question tags *That's right, isn't it?*

🐾 Subordinating conjunctions: A WHITE BUS

You can use the acronym **A WHITE BUS** to teach children the different subordinating conjunctions.

We couldn't go to the swimming pool because it was shut for repairs.

A	WH	I	T	E	B	U	S
although after as	when whenever whatever whether whereas which	if in order that in case	though till that	even if even though	because before	until unless	since